AND...SO WHAT?

Resilience Through Adversity

And...So What?
Resilience Through Adversity

A True Story By

JM VILLEGAS

Design SDA Creative
Copyright © JM Villegas
Ghostwriter Celina De León
Text is private and confidential
ISBN: 9798488191228

First print July 2021

www.andsowhat.online

CONTENTS

PROLOGUE — 7

1. NO TURNING BACK — 11

2. SHE IS GONE — 31

3. BOUNCING FROM WALL TO WALL — 49

4. LIVING IN THE FAST LANE — 61

5. "YES, SIR!" — 77

6. CRASH LANDING — 87

7. FRESH START — 95

8. PROCESSING IT ALL — 113

PROLOGUE

As life moves forward, more facts about its process reveal themselves and become apparent. Certainly, things fall into place, one way or another. However, one must always put in the work and break a sweat.

As a result, just one book dedication would have been very cliché. I feel gratitude to all who have positively contributed to my life's path and all the ways they have tried to insert their little piece of the big puzzle. My wife Krystyna has been a very important piece in my life. As the pieces have come together, it has been so great to see what picture my puzzle unfolds into and to remember how each piece formed that picture—each person who touched my life to bump me in the right direction.

Ironically, my mother initiated that journey in my life. First, by giving me the gift of life. Second, by giving me the great opportunity to conquer this life through hard work, struggle, and lessons that I otherwise would never have learned. After her tragic passing, the first piece of the puzzle was laid down on the table. One piece and no further clues.

Human lifelines are all filled with unexpected events. As a result, we can't escape loss, grief, pain, and other human experiences. But the timelines are different for everyone. Some of us live through these experiences early in life while others meet them later. Overcoming such events and experiences affects all of us in ways that perhaps we don't

AND... SO WHAT? RESILIENCE THROUGH ADVERSITY

understand in the moment—particularly at a young age, when these experiences essentially shape and mold the rest of a child's life. Behaviors and attitudes might appear out of the blue, and you may not even know where they came from.

Understanding tragedy and processing loss can take many years. In my case, it took 30 years to come to terms with it. Looking back, I can see now why, as a young boy, nothing had real meaning or made sense. It was unexplainable to someone looking from the outside. Just as I went through this, many others also navigate those rough waters at some point in their lives. Looking for immediate answers can be disappointing and can easily lead one in the wrong direction—down a path full of emotional barriers, disappointments, crossroads, and dead-end streets.

It is important to remember that our answers don't always come when we want them to. Sometimes they may not even come at all. But breaking through this is the real hope. What seemed like a consuming tragedy in due time looked more like a blessing. What seemed like a pit in due time looked more like a stepping stone across a wild river. However, the mind must be ready to recognize such reflection.

Enduring the challenge is part of the process, as is adapting to change, which is the key to overcoming any obstacle. If one thing is true, it's that no one has the answer to life's puzzles. The answer is within you and what you make of it.

Manny Villegas
Ontario, CA | February 2021

AND... SO WHAT? RESILIENCE THROUGH ADVERSITY

1

NO TURNING BACK

"Sometimes you just have to jump in the water. Don't waste your life thinking about it. Just do it."

I finally made it out of there. Alive. I was nineteen years old with no money in my pockets. My maternal grandmother, Marisol, asked me if I had any money when she dropped me off at the airport in Mexico City. Of course, I didn't. My pockets were empty. I was flat broke. I didn't even pay my aunt for the plane ticket her friend helped me get at the travel agency. Nevertheless, on September 26, 1998, my grandmother gave me the little money she had in her bank account and wished for God to give me the rest. She gave me a $100 jump-start. I was officially on my own and ready to hop onto a plane. My grandmother later passed away in the year 2010. She was never shy to share the little money she had with me or others.

Four hours later, I was in Los Angeles. An hour after that, I was at my paternal uncle's house with my aunt in Redondo Beach. I had no idea how long I was going to stay there because I had no idea when the job at my friend's uncle's

1. NO TURNING BACK

cell phone shop would begin. My friend was not returning any of my calls. What a flake, I thought. But I didn't care. I had what I needed—a roof over my head. I had a reason to leave everything that had been chasing me in Mexico City. I told my family I would be staying stateside for a couple of months. But deep down I knew better. There was no turning back. My new life was set to begin, but I needed to clear my head first. I needed to get away from all the partying, fighting, and distractions. I needed to get away from my family and from other people's rules and ideas about how to live my life. But I would need more time to get away from the latter. I needed a roof over my head first. And seeing that my friend still wasn't returning my calls, a job with my uncle was the next best thing.

My uncle had an old used furniture warehouse in downtown Los Angeles. It was a store that would have been lucrative in Mexico—where people regularly fixed things they found on the street and sold them for a decent price—where nothing went to waste. But that recycling mentality was not alive and well in L.A. when I arrived. So, I spent my days building wooden racks and welding a metal door that would always break. Moving furniture was a daily routine due to the water leaks in the building. We also had to deal with Skid Row, drug addicts, and the homeless. It was just the situation that surrounded the shop. We would often have to make sure that nothing was stolen. The shop was located on the ground floor of a cheap run-down motel on Seventh Street that brought all kinds of strange characters to the area. It was quite comical dealing with all those funny people, but we also had to watch our backs.

AND... SO WHAT? RESILIENCE THROUGH ADVERSITY

I worked during the day with my uncle and at some point took two classes at night—photography and swimming—at the nearby community college. My relatives had persuaded me, but I had no interest in their persuasive efforts whatsoever. I spent money that was meant for books on other interests, which got me in trouble with my aunt and uncle. But it was after swim class one night that my plans changed, yet again. Despite having no interest in the classes I was taking, I attended them, was on time, and got myself there and back on the bus or sometimes by bicycle. One night I missed the bus on the return. My paternal grandfather was visiting L.A. on business. I came out of swimming class late and missed the bus by a minute or two. It was around 9:15 at night, so I called for somebody to pick me up. It seemed simple enough. But something must have happened with the translation of my message. My relatives were upset and assumed I wasn't being responsible. Fortunately, my school was just ten minutes away from the house. But that didn't lessen the ordeal. To them, that was a big deal.

When I arrived at the house, the family was having dinner. Before I could even explain myself, the lecture ensued. "You need to be responsible. You are a disappointment. You need to be better!" I had left Mexico City to get away from all of this—the negative judgments and rules and everyone's different ways of living. Yet here I was—dealing with the same cages I had vowed to escape. What about how I wanted to live? I blew up.

"I've had it! I'm leaving." I immediately got up from the table and within five minutes I packed my things. I didn't have a lot to pack nor did I have a place to stay. Thankfully, my

1. NO TURNING BACK

uncle had bought me a 1970 Toyota Corona for $300. My first car! Not what I ever imagined my first car would be. It had rust everywhere but it drove OK despite the embarrassment. It would also serve as my home for the time being. Before I drove off, my grandfather was generous enough to give me $40. The journey on my own was now legit. I am grateful to my grandfather who believed in me. Days after leaving the house, he wrote me a letter that had so much wisdom to it. Grandpa passed away in the year 2000. I miss his wisdom and encouragement to always grab the bull by the horns. At this point, I had no idea where to go. I slept in my car for a couple of nights with all my physical and emotional baggage. I then called a friend I had just met a month before.

"Hey, man, I have good news. I'm going to stay with you." After his initial shock, he let me sleep on his couch for about a month or two. He had roommates to consider. My friend's couch was just what I needed to get my bearings. His roommates and I were all about the same age, which made me feel more at ease in that environment. I also noticed that they all worked and chipped in for rent and other household expenses. This was something I had to adapt to in order to continue sleeping on the couch for the time being.

I looked for jobs during the day and crashed on the couch at night. After looking and looking for whatever I could find, I landed a gig at the Redondo Beach Pier as a pizza guy. I made pizzas for seven dollars an hour. Despite the relief that came with finding an income, the job itself was depressing. I do not recommend working at a pier during winter. At the time, there were no customers, just cold waves crashing against the pier all evening. Sometimes I wondered if I should jump off

AND... SO WHAT? RESILIENCE THROUGH ADVERSITY

the pier for a cold swim and crash into those waves myself. I was that lonely and blue.

But I also knew deep in my heart that I had to push through. What other job can a nineteen-year-old without a college education get? I didn't have any other options so I had to make the best out of the opportunity I had. I lasted at the pizza place for a few months until I was fired for trying to survive. Working part-time while earning seven dollars an hour did not get me very far. I barely had enough money to pay my friend for a little rent and for gas to fill the tank of my embarrassing rusty car. Many nights I plain starved. But I learned very quickly that when you work in the food service industry, food is all around you. I eventually began saving customers' leftovers and also made pizzas to take home for dinner. I would make that pizza last for days. Unfortunately, that was my undoing. I got fired for making a pizza to take home with me at the end of my shift almost every day. That was my first time getting fired. Well worth it. I was now back to looking for work. I decided to stay with the food industry. I landed a job at Subway in Manhattan Beach. Fortunately, that area was popping with new restaurants coming in and out so there were plenty of places to pick up work. I eventually worked as a busboy in a sushi restaurant, as a cook in a teppanyaki restaurant, and whatever they needed at a sandwich shop. Anything that would pay the bills. I bounced all over the place trying to make a living. I found out early on that I had to work a lot to survive, but I still had a lot of fun doing it. I was finally free and the opportunities were endless.

All of my hard work eventually paid off. After a lot of hustle, I said goodbye to my friend's couch. I had saved

1. NO TURNING BACK

enough money to rent a bedroom in a house in Hawthorne. The guy that owned the house seemed to be professional and very inviting. But three months into my stay, I began to notice strange things happening on the property. I noticed more people coming around. Then I started to see drugs in plain sight. It wasn't my house, and I wasn't into drugs, so I kept to myself and tried not to be home. But then things got really crazy. Guns and cocaine were laid out on the kitchen table while the landlord had sex parties in the living room. That was definitely a situation I did not want to be a part of. But where was I supposed to go then? Thankfully, I had my car and could quickly put my clothes in a bag and take off. But where would I go?

Then one night while I was asleep, my landlord crept into my bed. It was 2:00 a.m. I wasn't fully awake. *Am I dreaming? What's going on?* My landlord was trying to sexually assault me! I kicked the sheets off and jumped out of bed. "What's going on here?!" I screamed. I then rushed to the bathroom and grabbed my phone. I was wearing a towel around my waist at this point because I was sleeping in my underwear. I then ran out and called the police. They arrested the landlord. I also found out that he was intoxicated at the time. It was very traumatizing, especially all the sexual assault questions and hospital tests they had me do. At some point it felt like an interrogation, like I was the criminal. Then they kept asking me about my family. "Where's your mother? Where's your father? You have no one in your corner?" These were uncomfortable questions I used to get asked frequently at a younger age, which I could never figure out how to answer.

After a couple of hours, I was finally allowed to go back

AND... SO WHAT? RESILIENCE THROUGH ADVERSITY

into the house and grab my belongings. I then called my aunt and uncle and told them what had happened. They were thankfully just ten minutes away and came to pick me up. Without reservation, they invited me back to their home. I went back. But I didn't stay very long because I didn't want to be engaged in any family rules. I wanted to be on my own. I had gone through a bad experience, but I couldn't sit back and wait for my life to begin. I needed to get out of there and continue with my life. I was determined to move forward.

 I stayed with my family for about three months. I continued working at Subway and other restaurants in that area and saved up enough money until I found a place of my own. It was about five minutes away in Redondo Beach. My very own studio apartment. 2200 Grant Avenue was my new home. This was such a simple but significant accomplishment for me at that time of my life. It wasn't just about having a place of my own but about being independent. I finally had peace to do what I wanted. And not because I wanted to go wild and party like crazy. I could now just come and go as I pleased without people telling me where to go, what to do, and how to do it. I could finally feel safe. Like no one was going to bother me or move me from my home because of someone else's reasons. I had finally found my little cave, my shelter. Mind you, I slept on the floor for a few months until I finally got a mattress. But that didn't bother me. What mattered was that I had made a big step in the direction that I wanted to go. A step that enabled me to continue being on my own, independent, and searching for what life had in store for me. I could now begin to plant the seed for my future. I was in bliss.

1. NO TURNING BACK

I started working at a Hawaiian furniture store in Manhattan Beach not too long after. This job was relatively close, it paid a bit better, and it gave me an opportunity to get a better car—a 1984 Volkswagen Rabbit GTI. This was a more reliable car that was decent and presentable because I now wanted to date, go out, and meet people. Now that I had some extra cash and my life was more stable, my age began to call for more. It wanted to explore my new freedom. But I didn't have a lot of time. I worked a lot, including weekends. I woke up at 4:30 a.m. to work at the furniture store's flea markets. While this did not leave me much time for rest, the extra money enabled me to feed myself, which was a relief and very significant for me because my childhood was much different. My mother and I didn't have many resources. Sometimes we would only have one piece of bread for dinner. So, it was a nice accomplishment for me to be able to consistently afford food and to be independent. My independence was priceless to me.

I budgeted carefully for groceries and did my shopping at the 99 Cent Store. I would go in with twenty dollars and know I could only buy nineteen items because of sales tax. I would buy a variety of food items. I had always been under somebody else's supervision or guidance, so I really didn't know what to buy. Or what I wasn't able to cook for myself. It was trial and error so many times. I was finally getting to know myself. My confidence was boosted every time I felt more independent and with stability came more and more freedom. The ability to do more and experiment with new things, like going to the beach, surfing, or just trying to figure myself out.

When I turned 21, I started drinking, legally. Not exces-

AND... SO WHAT? RESILIENCE THROUGH ADVERSITY

sively but quite often. I was going out to bars and hanging out with friends at the Hermosa Beach Pier. That's where the night life was happening. I would go there so often that I started to notice the same people over and over. We would hang out until late. Then I'd drive home. It was just a matter of time before I got in trouble. I think this was the very beginning of me trying to find ways to heal on my own. It's easy to judge someone when you're not in that person's shoes. You have no idea what most people are going through just by looking at them. Being in those shoes, you become your own reality. Alcohol during this time was a way for me to have a form of freedom to experience this stage of my life. It helped me to bring my mental and emotional defenses down so I could see who I was underneath all of my layers and guards. It allowed me to loosen up around people and to see another side of myself I didn't know. A part of myself that liked to be a little relaxed, a little more open. But I also found myself beginning to wonder how I could be that person without the buzz effect. I didn't necessarily like the outcomes.

Thankfully nobody got hurt, except for myself. Eventually my recklessness got me in trouble with the law. The first time… they made me go to classes and my license was suspended. The second time…six months later…I had to go to county jail. A sheriff pulled me over and ultimately handcuffed me and put me in the back of his car. I was so angry at him. I couldn't believe this was happening. Then I yelled, what seemed like out of nowhere at the time, "I hate you!" I was in shock. Where did that come from? He reminded me of a lifelong absent fatherly figure I never had. It was so strange. Something was boiling inside of me, and new feelings were

1. NO TURNING BACK

manifesting in my life. New truths were coming up for me that I knew I'd have to deal with soon.

I was put in a cell with other people. Real criminals. When they asked what I was in for, they just laughed. I got out the next morning. However, the judge ruled a few weeks later that because it was my second offense, I'd have to remain in jail for seven days. That was very scary. Forty people in a cell, all types of people in there, no separation, no nothing. It was quite something. Definitely not a joke. You really had to watch your back in there. You didn't have any friends inside. Literally. And there were all the rules you had to follow to not get hurt. For example, once inside you couldn't interact or talk to someone of a different race or color than you because your own people would take it as an offense. You definitely didn't want to offend anyone in jail. There was one toilet for all cell mates. During those long seven days, I took one shower and did not see the light of day. It was a very intense week.

But I am so grateful for the judge who made me go through this experience. He taught me a lesson alright! My mentality immediately changed once I was discharged. My decisions going forward moved me in a different direction. I was not the same person that I was going into jail, and I wasn't going to wait for the next changes to happen without putting out any effort. I was going to make them happen. As soon as I got out of county jail, I began looking for jobs. I really wanted to get out of the Hawaiian furniture store at this point. The couple who owned it had a very toxic relationship and it made the work environment toxic. They were always arguing and I did not want to be around that anymore. I'd been around that long enough as a child so I knew the potential aftermath.

AND... SO WHAT? RESILIENCE THROUGH ADVERSITY

I walked out of the store one day after they claimed to be better for me than my blood family. I blew up! They had no idea what they were talking about.

Around that time—I was somewhere between 21 and 22 then—I was in a relationship with a young woman I had met right before getting canned, who thankfully still stuck by me when I got out. She was surprisingly very understanding and really supportive of what I was going through. That to me was so important because, number one, I had no emotional support. Number two, I didn't have anyone around me who believed in me that thought I would become anything good or productive or positive. Understandably so. She was a breath of fresh air for me because I could finally rely on someone that was not judgmental toward what I was going through. There was hope for me now that there was somebody who actually believed in me and cared about what I was going through and didn't have something negative to point out about me. As a result, her positive support was critical to my growth. It really helped me to transition and to change the direction from where I was to where I wanted to go. It filled me with encouragement and motivation.

We met in 2001 and dated for a couple of years before we moved in together in 2003. At that point, I left the studio and we moved into a two-bedroom apartment. In 2004, we married. If I had been honest with myself, I knew deep down I wasn't ready for that commitment. That feeling became more urgent as time went by. Everything just seemed to be moving too fast for me. I started to feel a lot of pressure within. Primarily, I felt like I was finally starting to live my life and explore my freedom, but I had also made this huge

1. NO TURNING BACK

commitment. I began itching to travel and explore other interests. I hadn't done anything with my life yet and I wanted to do a million things. I felt anchored down by my own doing. She was a great person. I was just not in that state of mind. We amicably parted ways in 2009 and remain friends.

During our time together, I went back to college in 2002. I started taking online classes—just the basics. I also applied for twenty-plus jobs—anything that I could find. The college provided a job placement center, which I probably visited almost daily. A restaurant needed somebody to clean toilets?—I applied. They needed a baker?—Of course I can bake. Someone needed a janitor?—I'm your guy. Dishwasher?—When can I start? I applied for anything and everything because I needed to survive. If I didn't know how to do something, I was prepared to learn on my own and quickly. The need to survive makes a person grow, mature, and learn. It makes a person build a solid base for the future. This lesson has served me well throughout my life. I don't regret one job.

Fortunately, one of the jobs I applied for was at a hospital. It was an administrative assistant position. "Do you know anything about food services accounting?" I probably knew how to close out a register. My answer was "absolutely!" The job was for a food service administrative position in a hospital. Working at all those restaurants actually helped me acquire the experience I needed to land that job. Of course, I did not know this as I laid on my mattress feeling hopeless while I waited for the phone to ring. At that point I only had five dollars to my name. What was I going to do? Eat or pump gas? But the phone rang that evening and my five-dollar problem slowly disappeared. Now I just needed to figure out how to do the job. But wait—did I need to wear a tie? A suit? I had nothing to wear. I dressed the best I could with what I had until I got my first paycheck when I was finally able to buy office attire.

That's how I got into the business area of the medical industry, and I've been there ever since.

That job assisted me in more ways than one. In 2005, I took advantage of the hospital job's perks and got surgery by people I trusted. When I was nineteen, I tore my ACL ligament. I got the ACL repaired and all the while did not miss a single class of college. I still drove to school and hobbled on crutches to all of my classes with a cast on my leg. It was a challenge, and it was very painful. But I couldn't afford to get behind because I did not want to postpone graduation. I needed to graduate as soon as possible for my life to keep progressing in the right direction. So, I didn't quit any of my classes, not even calculus. I just kept going.

I worked full-time and went to school full-time. I was determined to do well and graduate. For five years I followed the same routine. I worked from nine to five during the day and went to school from six to ten at night. I would then go home and do homework for the following day until midnight or one o'clock in the morning. I'd wake up, and do it all over again.

It's funny…despite my exhaustion. I never really thought about giving up. I just didn't think I had that option.

I was determined and I didn't stop once. I was all in for five years. I finished college with no debt or loans to pay. I barely made it through those years.

I studied business administration and marketing. I come from a long line of business people, so it's in my blood. But

1. NO TURNING BACK

I'm also creative, which is what drew me to marketing and advertising. I had two very good professors who made an impact on me. The first one was my marketing and advertising professor. He was a young guy but a very wise person. I've always gravitated toward wise people because they must have gone through something to learn what they know. I've always tried to apply their lessons as a result. One of his lessons that always stuck with me was "Don't be that person who over promises because you will under deliver." He said it as simple as that. This important rule applies to so many situations. It can be as simple as when you tell someone that you will call him or her back in five minutes even though you know you're not going to. Give yourself time instead and avoid causing unnecessary disappointment. The same rule applies to work projects.

Don't over promise to a client because you will be stuck under delivering and have an unhappy client. It's such a simple yet important rule that a lot of people take for granted. As a result, I make sure to be careful with my words now.

The other professor that had a real impact on me was my law professor, who was a practicing attorney. I admired her because she was very straightforward, very tough, but also very funny. She always had really good advice on how to deal with a variety of situations, such as how to deal with attorneys and how to participate in certain legal cases. To this day, I still apply what I learned in that class. Having that legal knowledge has been a real asset to my career.

I graduated magna cum laude in 2007 from California State in Dominguez Hills with a Bachelor's degree in Business Administration and Marketing. I invited only my aunt and uncle since they were local. In the past, I had heard people around me say that the odds were against me. That my life would not amount to anything. I understand why. It definitely seemed that way—that I would be a criminal or locked up in prison. I was told, literally, that the odds that I would achieve anything in my life were very low if things in my life didn't change. For me to be able to reach that accomplishment, to graduate college on my own, was its own self reward. I learned over time that I didn't have to prove anything to anybody. That to me was the most rewarding gift. I proved to myself, no one else, that I was and am capable of doing amazing things.

My motto ever since has been to keep going, keep pushing. Even if you don't know where you're going, you must push. Even if you don't know your destination, just keep pushing forward because something has to come up. An opportunity is bound to come your way. But you have to keep moving forward in a positive direction in order to grab those opportunities. Don't become complacent. And in trying to develop yourself, in trying to better yourself, something is going to give. There is no way it won't happen. The ability to catch this opportunity will be all on you. You must be prepared. Then, I could only rely on myself moving ahead. I was determined to do so.

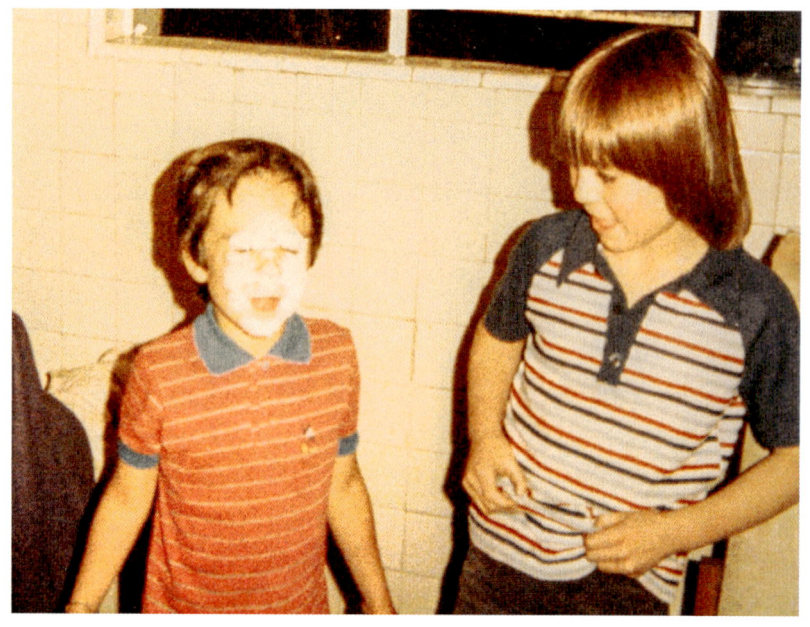

My friend Maurcio and I as kids. We remain friends to this day.

My first car. 1970 Toyota Corona.

My Grandma and I at the airport during one of many visits to Mexico City.

Fixing an old kawasaki bike.

Grandma Marisol's home in Mexico City.

Grandpa, my cousin Mily and I having a good time 1988.

My classmates in middle school in Mexico City 1991.

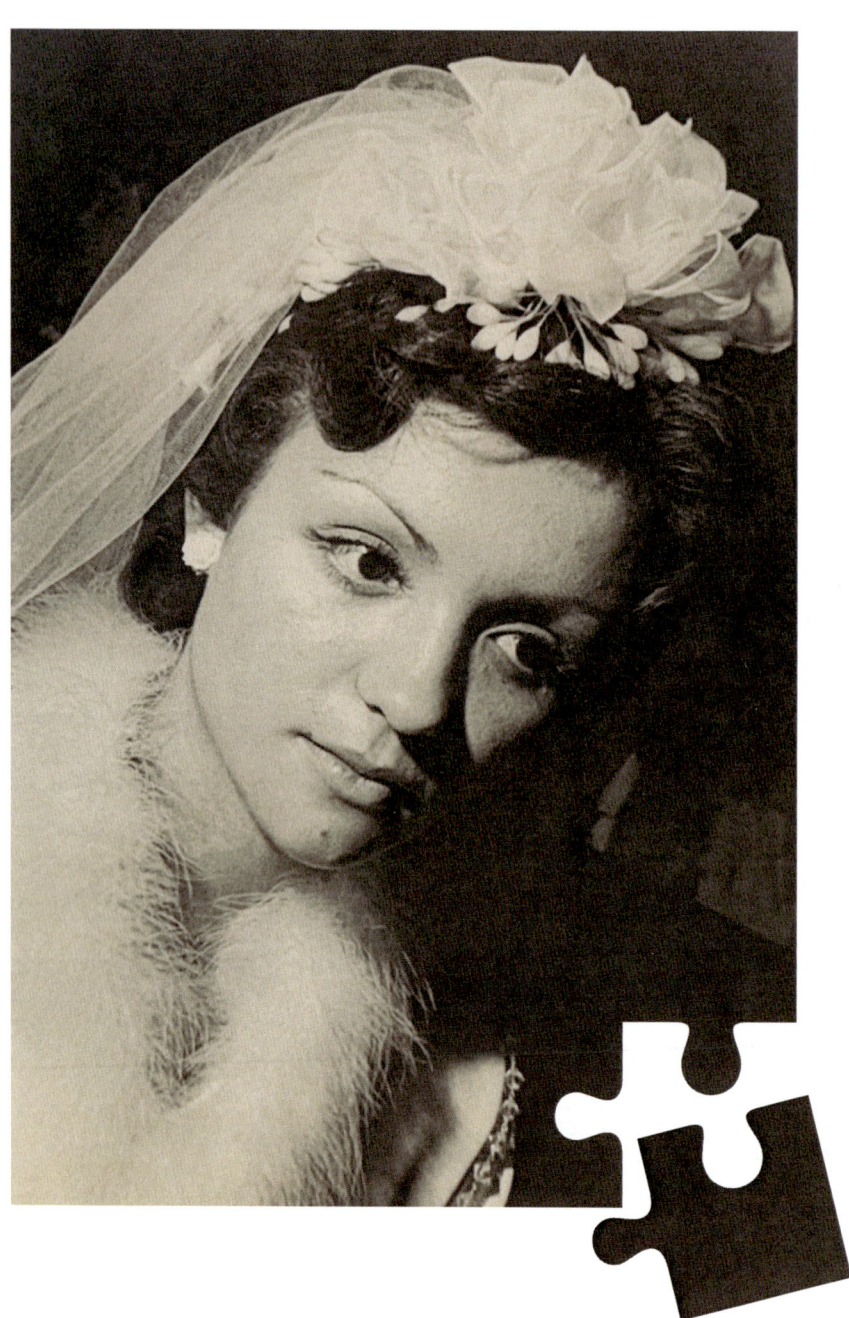

"One piece, and no further clues."

2

SHE IS GONE

"Don't expect to understand life. You simply won't. No matter what...keep your chin up and push ahead."

My earliest memory as a child is with my mother. She was making animated faces at me as I lay in my cradle. So typical of my mother. I was born in Mexico City, a very Colonial city with many Spanish and French European influences. My mother was born in Mexico City, as well, and named after her mother, Marisol. She gave birth to me when she was nineteen years old. My mother was very loving and caring with me and very playful. We would play all sorts of games together. She even made a game out of teaching me English. I'd make up words and pretend they meant something. Despite my noninterest in learning any language, we had so much fun. My mother would also make funny faces all the time. She was very animated. I loved to make faces back at her. We would laugh a lot.

My mother was beautiful, charismatic, and outgoing. She was also very nontraditional for a woman of her time. She was not afraid of getting dirty, jumping fences, roller

2. SHE IS GONE

skating, riding bicycles and motorcycles, or taking risks. But she also had a very artistic, creative side. She would make little works of art out of pieces of wood and Styrofoam. She would sit and patiently draw, paint, and glue them together into intricate figurines. During Christmas we would all look forward to the ornaments and little ornate boxes she would make, sell, or give away. I think I got my crafty, handy spirit from her. I always have a project around the house that I am working on. My wife calls me the "raccoon."

Around the time I was two or three years old, my mother moved us in with her mother, my grandmother. My mother also had a sister she was close to, Aunt Carmen, who lived nearby. We had a nice life together. It was comfortable and safe. My grandmother always had enough food at the house. We had all that we needed.

When my mother was in her early 20s and I was about four or five, she began to date a young man named Juan. He was two years her junior. The surrounding peace we had enjoyed soon came crashing to an end. Juan was shaky and had high, intense energy. He wasn't stable financially or otherwise. He was a drifter who never knew where his next paycheck would come from. He mostly lived off of my mother's salary as a government entry-level secretary and never helped my grandmother with the groceries he ate. Our peaceful home became very intense. There was now always animosity and tension in the air and arguments brewing. At one point he had a gun in the house, and it just wasn't a safe environment around him. He had pointed the gun at my grandmother and this had become a huge issue. This would cause us to move out, with no place to go.

AND... SO WHAT? RESILIENCE THROUGH ADVERSITY

Then one day my mother and I left with Juan for La Paz on the peninsula of Los Cabos for a few months. It wasn't very clear why we left my grandmother's comfortable home to live in a small motel in some rural area. There was a farm nearby where Juan and my mother dropped me off before they went to work during the day. Despite being of school age, I was not enrolled and was left to hang out by myself with people at the farm. I remember the motel was long and dark, and we lived in the last room at the very end to the far right. It was in a very rural area with dirt roads and mud all around. I remember not wearing shoes at the time and getting my feet all dirty. I didn't really have the disposition to say anything or give my opinion at five years old. I just went along with whatever they were doing, wherever they were taking me. They both worked an ice-cream truck around the small city. It was a very odd situation. I remember one day at the beach, at sunset, Juan offered me beer and got me drunk. I was just a child. I don't recall much about it. We lived in La Paz for about six months before moving back in with my grandmother in Mexico City.

A few months after that, my mother finally saved up enough money to rent her own place. It was a little one-bedroom apartment. Despite its small size, its ceilings were almost chapel-like and very colonial looking. My mom was excited about decorating it, making it feel like a home. She picked up a can of pink paint and we painted half of the apartment together. I can still remember the smell of the paint as we brushed the walls. We didn't have any furniture—just our two beds that were placed in the bedroom. The apartment came with a stove. We had some basic silverware

2. SHE IS GONE

and a small table to eat at. No television or radio. Just very basic necessities.

The apartment was a big accomplishment for my mom. She was 29 and really valued her independence. She was also starting to make some extra money now, enough to pay for rent and some food. Instead of contributing to the household, Juan took whatever was left for job hunting and his other personal matters. He continued not being stable and picked up odd jobs here and there. Including a job at a famous restaurant in Mexico City called "La Casa Morada" that was shut down a couple of times after being raided for drug trafficking. The family suspected Juan was involved in some strange drug deals. With Juan always in between jobs and my grandmother no longer in the picture, we often did not have enough to eat. I remember walks by myself to the local bakery with just a couple of pesos to spend. I would buy three pieces of bread. Typically French Rolls or "Bolillos." That would be our lunch and our dinner for the day. I was hungry quite often.

As time went on, our lives only got worse at the apartment. The tension began to escalate, and Juan became more and more volatile. Our new life together went downhill very fast, very badly. Every morning my mother left for work dressed nicely for her office job, only to return home in the evening to Juan's jealous rages. And then all hell would break loose overnight. Constant arguments, yelling and screaming to no end.

With no grandmother to check him, Juan's temper became explosive and his abuse overt. The first few times he yelled and screamed at my mother. Then he pretty much controlled every movement she made. He had rules for what

AND... SO WHAT? RESILIENCE THROUGH ADVERSITY

she could wear, who she could talk to, and that he had to pick her up from work—even though they didn't own a car. What an insecure loser! Then Juan began to grab, shove, and push my mother. I remember one time when Juan and my mother were fighting in the very small kitchen. Only four people could fit into it. Very quickly their fight got out of hand. So much so that Juan attacked my mother physically by shoving and grabbing her. My mother threw some knives at him in defense. I saw it all—they did not censor themselves. They were not concerned with the possible impact this violence would have on me in years to come. It's as if I became invisible in their rage. I was just seven years old—a sponge with no filter.

Things went on like that for a while. Then Juan started to physically abuse me. I remember one instance when we were all at the grocery store with Aunt Carmen. I was fooling around with the supermarket cart, like all kids inevitably do when they are left unsupervised. Eventually, I accidentally hit Juan's heel with the cart. This grown man did not hesitate to turn around and violently punch me in the stomach—a child's stomach. The world went black and all the air in my lungs escaped me. I gasped for air. I fainted. It took me a while to recover. I came back to my mother and Aunt Carmen yelling at Juan, "What the hell were you thinking?" Without skipping a beat, Juan responded, "Well, he clipped me with the cart." He was 27 at the time, and I was seven. That was the first time I was punched, and I was punched by an adult, many times my size. A bully. The warning signs that something was terribly wrong continued.

One of the next beatings was at home. He terrorized

2. SHE IS GONE

me after picking me up from school for misbehaving. Again, what seven-year-old does not misbehave in school at some point? During the whole ride on the public bus home, he injected fear in me. He psychologically tortured me by describing how he was going to beat me with a broomstick. When we got home, that's exactly what he did. He beat me with a broomstick handle so bad that it left marks all over my body. When my mom got home, she was upset. She screamed at Juan, "What the hell are you doing to my son?"

Despite my mother's protests, the violence continued with no relief in sight. I can't count how many times I saw my mother slapped or punched in the face, without any remorse by Juan. These fights just got more and more "normal" and became more and more violent and brutal. They were constantly happening. One time, after all the grabbing and punching, my mom tried to run out the door. She almost made it out, but when she was halfway through, Juan ran and kicked the door and smashed my mom between the door and the wall. I can still remember that image to this day…Juan dragging my mother's body back into the apartment. How much more ruthless could Juan get? At this pace, something was bound to happen.

The aftermaths of these fights would not be any less brutal. My mother would be bleeding, with her face covered in bruises. Juan would instruct her without question, without any remorse, to tell people at work that we were all playing soccer and the ball had hit her face. My mother was very proud and wouldn't want people judging her and telling her what to do. But her pride only further isolated her. She saw less and less of my grandmother and Aunt Carmen as a result. My grandmother was still working at the time and would drive my mother to work in the morning and me to school. The mornings my mother woke up all black and blue she would tell my grandmother not to pick her up. We would take the bus. My mother kept everything to herself. But my grandmother suspected odd things were going on though she could not imagine the level of violence that existed in that apartment. After paying for all his meals and living with him those months, my grandmother never warmed up to Juan. Deep down she knew he was sketchy. At one point, my Aunt Carmen went so far as to offer my mother and me a place to stay in her house. My mother didn't take the offer. I think she thought she could still control the situation on her own. But the fights only got more frequent and more intense.

    Juan even went so far as to call a meeting about what was allowed during those fights. I remember the three of us sitting on the beds as Juan led the discussion. One of the main things Juan discussed was that my mother could not attempt to take her life during their disputes. That's because he was fully aware that my mother was suicidal. That she was trapped and desperate for a way out and that my mother had tried cutting her wrists a couple of times before. On a couple of occasions I had seen for myself my mom holding a knife to her wrist and Juan struggling to take it away from her. Looking back, it is perverse and sickening that the person who beat my mom prevented her from doing something more than that to herself. No matter what, my mother had to endure Juan's beatings. But despite Juan's insistence, my mom always said she could not guarantee that she would not take her own life. It almost seemed like her mind was made up.

2. SHE IS GONE

The last fight they had was roughly two weeks before my mother's 30th birthday. I was eight years old then. I never knew what the motive of the fight was. There was grabbing, shoving, and punching, to say the least. Juan had her pinned down on the bed, on top of her, and punched her on the face with no remorse. It was horrifying as a child to see this and feel powerless. Tension and fear consumed the apartment. It was hell, but I didn't know it at the time. I could only feel the fear. After the tempo and intensity had mellowed a bit, my mom went into the bathroom, which was inside the one bedroom we all shared. I followed her into the bathroom and looked up at my mother's face. I saw that she had just taken down a big bottle of pills. My eight-year-old self did not question why she was taking those pills in that manner. Why would she? I was young and innocent. I did not understand what her actions meant or what the consequences of her actions would be. I still wonder, though, what my mother thought the moment she put that bottle down and saw me looking up into her eyes. Her bruised face looking down at me, expressing dismay and doubt, but she also appeared to be trapped in fear. She then went to bed.

It did not take much time for my mom to be in a comatose state. At that point, it was nighttime. We had turned off the lights and all gone to bed. But Juan kept talking and rambling. He then noticed that my mother was not responding. The only thing she could do was moan at that point. By the time Juan realized what was happening, that my mother was not well, that her light was flickering out, he panicked. Finally, he had me turn on the light. My mother was still making noises, but her eyes were now in the back of her head. Juan turned to me and asked, "What happened? What did she do?" I told him what I had seen, which I didn't know was bad. That my mother had swallowed some pills. Juan then sat my mom up at the side of the bed and placed a bucket in front of her and tried to make her vomit. Before I knew it, tons of white pills poured out of my mom's mouth. I couldn't believe nor understand what I was seeing. The room stank horribly. The sight of white pills and vomit all over the floor and my unconscious mother's clothes was horrifying.

 Juan had tried to make my mom vomit as much as possible, but the pills had already entered her bloodstream. My mother had lost consciousness and was now not making a sound. She needed an ambulance and we did not own a phone. There was a pay phone at the pharmacy catty-corner to our apartment building. Juan yelled for me to call for help. From the moment I ran out the door and the moment I arrived at the pay phone, it was all a blur. But the feeling I felt when I realized I could not reach the phone to call for help for my mother is something I will never forget. My stomach sank! I felt so helpless! It was late at night. There was no one around and I could not reach the phone no matter how many times I tried. I couldn't do anything. I was powerless.

 I ran back to the apartment and explained to Juan what had happened. We then grabbed my mom and laid her down on the bed. She was still breathing but she was consciously gone. My mother was not there. Juan then began rubbing alcohol on her forehead. I guess he was following some grandmother's recipe to keep her awake by the smell or coldness of the alcohol. I grabbed a piece of cardboard that was lying around and waved air in her face as Juan left to call

2. SHE IS GONE

for an ambulance. I kept waving air into her face…her eyes were rolled back…and talking quietly by her side until he returned. "Mom, are you OK? Please wake up." It was such a scary moment knowing that she was fading away and that there was nothing I could do. At the same time, I wished that she was joking with me and that she would open her eyes and scare me with one of her animated faces. Part of me hoped that would happen. But Juan returned and I kept blowing air into her face as she was whisked away into the ambulance.

We flew through the streets to the hospital. I can barely remember the ride. Before I knew it, Juan and I were sitting in the emergency waiting room, and he was telling me to pray for my mother. "You need to pray that she's going to be OK." I was eight years old and did what he told me to do. But then he started asking me what he should do after he was done praying. How would I know? I was a child. But he was relentless. "What should I do? Should I call your grandmother? Should I call your grandfather?" My mother was dying and this man was asking me, her eight-year-old son, what he should do. I told him to make the calls. I didn't know what to do but even I knew he should at least do that.

My grandmother and Aunt Carmen arrived. So did my maternal grandfather. They all wanted to know what had happened. But Juan was adamant that we hide the truth. He insisted that I not say anything to anybody. Like he did with my mother, he brainwashed and manipulated me to hide the truth. As family members kept arriving and trying to figure out what had put my mother in such a predicament, I was forced to say I didn't know. Overall, things did not look good. Some family members even tried to distract me for my own good by taking me to eat something. I had been there for almost 24 hours with no food.

I was told the doctors did all they could for my mom. They did an internal wash of her stomach and intestines, but it was too late. Too much time had passed since she had ingested the pills. The medication from all the pills had already reached her bloodstream and got to her brain, which caused her to have a brain hemorrhage. My mother laid in that hospital for a day or two before she was transferred to another hospital. She stayed there for a bit, but there was nothing they could do, either. My mother, Marisol, died on January 30, 1987.

When my paternal family broke the news to me that my mom had passed away, I didn't understand what that meant. When they told me she went to heaven, to a better place with a huge garden and lots of flowers, it sounded nice. It seemed like a good thing so I figured it was best for her be there. I was like "OK" and shrugged my shoulders up and down. I did not comprehend the meaning of death at that age. That I would never get to talk to her again. That I would never see her again. That my family members were trying to make the death of my mother easier. Not understanding the concept of death would prove to be difficult for me. As a result, for many years, I had so many unanswered questions. I could not grasp the whole idea or understand what had happened to her and what had happened to me. It took many years for me to process the grief I could not understand back then. How can you explain grief to a child? Or loss? How do you even explain the emotions associated with those events? The process had to be discovered through time, processed and

2. SHE IS GONE

healed over many years. I had to learn to understand the loss of my mother and the loss of my childhood.

I remember little about the funeral. I don't know who arranged it. There were even some people from my mom's work, I was told. It was all a blur. I remember one day visiting her grave, knocking on my mother's grave. "Mom, are you there?" Looking back at this as an adult, I can only imagine how heartbreaking that must have been for my family members. Looking at this child, unfamiliar with the term "death," as he hopes to have a response back from his mother's grave. The truth was that I had never heard of death before the death of my mother. I had no idea the powerful and detrimental impact her death would have on me in years to come. Unfathomable to anyone looking from the outside.

All in all, I had to grow up very fast. See, every person has a story, a past, a struggle, a loss. The timelines of such events might be different for all, some early in life, some later in life. But they can definitely affect each one of us very differently, depending on when such things happen. As a child, when life is new and nothing makes sense, those types of events can be very difficult to understand. However, the expectation coming from an adult's perspective can underestimate what this child might have to go through to understand and overcome such a tremendous loss, if not the biggest loss of all.

From left to right - Grandma Rachel, My mother Marisol carrying me, and Grandpa Villegas. Picture in Spain around 1979.

My aunt Carmen with Grandma Marisol at her home in Mexico City.

> *Mandolito*
> *Querido Hijo:*
>
> 14 Junio 1981
>
> Espero siempre conserves estas fotografías que son de la etapa mas bella del Humano la "infancia" para que el día de mañana lo hagas al igual que yo lo he hecho con Amor, con el anhelo de darte lo mejor de la vida, de la ternura al tenerte en mi brazos, delocairnos que siempre has sido de lo maravilloso que es oír de ti la palabra "mamá" o mamita, pero quiero que sepas también que llegara el día en que tu formarás tu familia porq'así debe de ser, ya que eres mi hijo que yo te concebí, te dí la vida te vi nacer, y te vi crecer y desarrollarte, mas no me perteneces por q' cada humano, tiene su personalidad, su carácter su individualidad
>
> tu mamá te quiera siempre
> Manuel M.

This letter was written in 1981 by my mother, years before her tragic passing, it seems to convey words with great wisdom. She instinctively delivered an early message as if she knew she wouldn't be around for me in years to come. See translation, next page top right.

◀ *Translation:*

Dear Son,

I hope you always keep these pictures that belong to the most beautiful part of life of a human being, the "childhood". The hope is that one day you can do the same, as I have done this for you. With love and with the desire to give you the best of life, with the tenderness to have you in my arms, as sweet as you have always been and how marvelous it is to hear the words, "Mom" or "Mommy". But, I also want you to know that there will come a day that you will form your own family, because that's how life is supposed to be. You are my son, I gave birth to you, I gave you life, I saw you grow and develop; however, you don't belong to me. Every human being has their own personality, character, and individuality.

Your mother will always love you.
Marisol M

Visiting some beach on a trip with my mother.

Always thoughtful.

My mother somewhere in Spain during her few travels.

Two of the most influential people in my life. My mother and Grandpa.

My mother's wedding day.

Spain. It seems like there was always something in her mind.

3

BOUNCING FROM WALL TO WALL

"Throughout your journey, keep in your heart what brings you good; the rest you can leave behind."

Despite what people around me said, I was not an orphan. I never felt like one nor did I ever ask to be treated like one. But after my mother's passing, I was told I would be living with my paternal grandparents in Mexico City. Juan had cleaned out my mother's apartment and left nothing for me to keep. Not even my mother's jewelry. I now had to start a new life without her. My grandparents were chosen because they were stable and offered to take the parenthood lead. Moving in with my grandparents would prove to be a good distraction from the grief, but it would eventually catch up with me.

Looking back, what a challenging job my grandparents took on…taking care of an eight-year-old who had just lost his mother and who had already experienced so much trauma. They stepped up and took me in. They loved me very much.

My grandfather was still working at the time. He was a

3. BOUNCING FROM WALL TO WALL

business owner who had worked his whole life. Overnight I went from being of very poor socioeconomic status, of sometimes just eating a piece of bread for dinner, to living in a big house with a big garden, several cars, my own room, and plenty of food to eat. Thankfully, that home would provide me with many good memories. Just what I needed at the time—a normal, stable life.

My grandparents were very, very loving, as well as very, very disciplined. I learned that right away. My grandfather initiated me into learning how to work. Not just to work but how to get into the mindset of work. He wisely taught me that I was going to have to work, and as a result, I was going to need to learn the responsibility of having a job. To this day, that's probably one of the best lessons that I've learned in my life. I'm so grateful to have been able to learn that discipline at a very early age—to learn what work means and what having that responsibility means.

In my new life with my paternal grandparents I would go to school, like a normal kid, Monday through Friday. Then on Saturdays I would work at my grandfather's huge warehouse where he sold office furniture. To be honest, half the time I was playing around and having fun riding around the warehouse on a pallet jack like a scooter. My grandfather would get mad at me and yell at me from across the way. He did give me job responsibilities, and eventually I did them. I would have to count 100 screws and put them in a bag and then count 100 nuts and then put them in a bag as well. I don't know how reliable my math was, but I did what I could. Sometimes my job would be to sweep the floor. Sometimes my job would be to clean the furniture with a rag and some special spray. At the time, all of those jobs were tedious and boring and I didn't like them. But looking back, I can see he gave me those jobs so I could learn that jobs require the fulfillment of certain responsibilities. I think learning this lesson from a very early age gave me an advantage in many ways to be able to adapt in my career and have a competitive advantage. I didn't see responsibilities as "this is not what I like to do…this is not what I signed up for." Instead of behaving like the job owed me, I saw those challenges as ways to adapt, grow, and ultimately find new opportunities. That is how I've been able to reach my goals.

My grandfather would reward me with a twenty pesos bill here and there. It wasn't something I ever expected. I actually enjoyed our time together on Saturdays, during our drives on the way to work and on the way back home. We would occasionally eat somewhere together. On Sundays, we enjoyed soccer. I belonged to a soccer club. My team was Rio Covadonga, named after a community located in Asturias, Spain. My grandfather, of Spaniard heritage, was a "futbol" fanatic and my biggest fan. It was funny to see him enjoying the game from the bleachers and then to talk to him after the game. Sometimes it felt like I was talking to another kid. "Hey, did you see when I did this dribble?" Of course he did, and he loved it! It was nice to have that bond with him. I felt like he was my friend, somebody I trusted, and somebody I felt comfortable with. We had a really good vibe going.

We played all types of games together. My grandfather taught me how to play dominoes. We would play before we went to sleep. We would set up the game at the kitchen table and joke around about cheating. He liked to cheat sometimes

3. BOUNCING FROM WALL TO WALL

to beat me. I would also do the same. But our favorite game was Uno. Sometimes at night, not every night, if he wasn't too tired after work, we'd play a game before he went to sleep. He would lay in his bed and I would kneel on the side of the bed. He would pretend to fall asleep and drop about five cards. I would say, "Hey, are you cheating? What happened to your cards?" He would playfully say, "I'm so sorry. I was falling asleep." He would play with me like that, and we would laugh so hard! The old man really cared for me. It was a very different vibe from my time with Juan. Grandpa wanted to help me grow and prepare me for life, and so he did. I miss the old man.

My grandfather also taught me how to make omelets, which would prove to be a handy survival skill later in life. He called them "tortilla de huevo." Eggs were cheap and you could put anything in them. Every morning my grandfather and I would make an omelet together. It was our routine, and it was fun because we always made a different concoction. One morning we'd add some bell peppers and onions to our omelets. The next morning we'd put some chorizo, olives, and cheese—whatever we would find in the fridge.

Our routine life together made me feel like a normal kid. He fulfilled a paternal role with me. I didn't have to worry about my well-being, and I felt safe and secure. I also got to go to the same school for the remainder of the year that I was going to when my mom was still alive. That was great for me, but for my grandparents it meant a 45-minute drive each way. My paternal Aunt Rachel lived next door to my grandparents and she would sometimes take me to school and help my grandparents take care of me. All uncles and aunts contributed in one way or another as much as they could.

But I still felt drawn to preserving my life with my mom. I was still attached to the past. When I first moved in with my grandparents, Juan came to visit me a few times. Then my grandparents thought it would be best that he didn't. Getting adjusted to living with my grandparents was difficult. I was so attached to my mother and I was so attached to Juan. Despite all of his abuse, he was the only thing I knew. He was my family, so I wanted to continue my relationship with him, unfortunately. I began to sneak phone calls to him in my grandparents' bedroom. I would whisper, "Hey, how are you? What's going on? Yeah, can you come and see me?" I would always ask him to take me somewhere because I thought, and felt, that somehow I was connected to my mother through my relationship with him. How could I have known better?

But my calls to Juan got so crazy that my grandparents had to make a very tough decision. They forbade me from calling Juan anymore and placed little locks on the dials of the phones so I couldn't dial out. I flipped out. "No, you can't do this to me!" I was really sad for a while. I cried and cried. I just couldn't understand why they were doing this to me.

All in all, I was feeling out of place in some way or another, and I was just missing the presence of my mother. Even though I knew she wasn't there with him, Juan made me feel a sense of comfort because he represented my relationship with my mother. When my grandparents stopped my communication with Juan, it felt like the world had ended because that was the only thing that was left that made me feel close to my mother. At some point, Juan simply represented some sort of a hope that I would see my mother

3. BOUNCING FROM WALL TO WALL

again. When I was told to let go of this hope, it meant having no hope. It was a very difficult thing for me to accept and to take in. Ultimately, it was best for me, without a doubt. After a while, the need to call Juan sort of faded away. That need was filled by other distractions, such as a new school, new friends, some discipline, and extracurricular activities. They started to fill the void and allowed me to let go of my old situation a bit.

I was able to see my grandmother, my aunt Carmen, and my cousin on my mom's side. Grandma Marisol would come and visit me. I would go on outings with her for the day or for maybe a couple of days. I would pack my bags and go to my other grandmother's house where I could just hang out. That was nice. But I would always have to come back and start my routine all over again with my grandparents. And it was nice to be able to do that, too.

At home, my grandfather was very kind and loving, but he was not sweet. He was rough around the edges. He would wake me up in the morning by pulling my ear, nose, or toes! I think he was rough because he experienced a similar loss at a young age. His mom and his sister were killed in a car accident, getting hit by a train. He saw his dead mom's body in the wreckage. As a result, I think he understood my situation and may have seen himself in me in his younger years. I think this may have bonded us more than anything because we had a very special bond. He didn't talk about his feelings—he was more a person of action. But because of his rough parts he was able to talk about tough stuff. Looking back, he was very different with me than he was with his kids…all of my uncles and aunts. He was very rough, very tough, and very strict with them. But I also think, because our backgrounds were similar enough, that he knew he had to be a little bit softer, a little bit more tender with me. I am glad he was.

Grandma Rachel also had her strict rules. I had to study for hours and do my homework. I had to clean my shoes on Friday to get them ready for the following week. I wasn't allowed to put my elbows on the table. I wasn't allowed to sing at the table. My grandmother always said, "There's a place and a time for everything." I am grateful now for those ways that they taught me. Especially in this day and age, when it is hard to find people practicing manners or simple consideration for others. Those are priceless values that I inherited and took with me that I will most likely pass on to my own kids. Probably not as strict in some ways…because times have changed…but I think those values are something to live by.

At the same time, my grandparents made sure I had time to hang out with a friend or two. They didn't give me extreme discipline. For me, coming from a home filled with lots of chaos, there was no discipline, only reprimands. Chaos meant I was either verbally abused or physically abused by Juan. It wasn't about giving me a structure and a foundation to live by. It was about putting fear in me. By comparison, my grandparents had people help around the house during the week. So, my grandmother said that on the weekends I had to make my bed. Little things like that. It wasn't so much about the complexity of the task but about understanding responsibility. And that was really good for me. It was a wise practice.

While my mother was playful when she tried to teach me

3. BOUNCING FROM WALL TO WALL

English, my paternal grandmother was the total opposite. She meant business. She wanted me to learn the language properly. She would sit down with me and read in English. When she heard me speak English, which was definitely not English, she would exclaim, "Oh my God, what are you saying?" It was quite funny actually. My grandmother was a proud American-born citizen and we would take trips to McAllen, Texas, quite often to vacation and visit her sister. During those trips it was easier to start picking up English. I was traveling a bit more, which was something that I had rarely done, but it was fun. I remember how excited I was to be on a plane. But then I would look over at my grandmother and she would say, "Let's say a prayer before the airplane takes off." I would pray with her even though I found it funny and cute.

At that point in my life, I felt like my grandmother and my grandfather were my parents because they took care of me as parents would. Their home felt like my home. The drawback? It was very short-lived. I was only with them for about a year and a half. My honeymoon period with them came to an end. When I was nine or ten years old, I started acting out more and having big flare-ups and tantrums—the kind where you can't really communicate what you're feeling but you have stuff going on. I really didn't know why I was acting out. I couldn't explain it. At some point, they took me to a child psychologist. I specifically remember the psychologist giving me a little toy gun with darts. The psychologist said, "Grab the gun and just play with it. OK, now shoot." Then the psychologist grabbed a doll and said, "Pretend that's your grandmother. What would you do?" I looked at her and thought, "Are you crazy?—I'm NOT going to shoot my grandmother!—Are you out of your mind? It was all very strange. At a certain point I began to question why I was going to play with this psychologist. I was also starting to grasp the idea that, inside me, something was starting to turn on. I was going through so much and my family knew that I had gone through a lot, but they didn't know all the violence and trauma I had been through, or all that was going on inside me—and neither did I. That is something I have talked about very little in my life until now in this book.

Why was I changing then? I didn't understand. I was taking the bus to and from school and I began to miss it intentionally. I walked home a few times as a result. My behavior was changing and none of us knew why. Looking back, I thought I would be with them forever. But, at the same time, they were older. My paternal grandparents were both in their 70s and couldn't keep up with me at this stage in my life. I remember my grandmother explaining how she was tired and how she didn't have the same energy like somebody younger had. She teared up as she explained this to me but she was very sweet about it. At some point, they decided that the best place for me was under paternal care in McAllen, Texas. This time of my life would turn out to be my loneliest and most isolated time as a child. But fortunately, it was short-lived. My time in Texas came to an abrupt end very quick.

Grandpa and I at the dining table playing around. I'm listening to some rock music most likely.

When I was 9 versus when I was in my mid twenties, sitting at my aunt Rachels stairs.

My paternal grandparents.

From left to right - grandma Rachel, myself and grandma Marisol at a 6th grade school gathering.

4

LIVING IN THE FAST LANE

"The excitement of living in the fast lane goes away very quickly when you realize your brakes don't work and the wall is coming at you fast."

Once again I was on the move. I was sent back from McAllen to Mexico City but to live with my maternal grandmother who had recently retired. She had the time to spend with me but she was not as financially stable as my paternal grandparents were, even though she always made sure I was well fed and had the things I needed and sometimes more. I was then eleven or twelve years old, back in Mexico City, with no friends, in unfamiliar turf, and once again adapting to a new socio-economic environment.

My maternal grandmother was very loving and caring. But she sometimes also had a very strong character and was strict in some of her ways. I came to realize during my time with her that everyone had his or her own set of beliefs and not everyone was as flexible or accepting of other ways of doing things. And that, largely, those ways of doing things were instilled at childhood and how someone was raised. As

4. LIVING IN THE FAST LANE

a result, everyone around tried to infuse their knowledge and experience into me and pass on their beliefs. I encountered many schools of thought. At times, I felt like an experiment for all those different opinions. Adaptation would prove time and again to be the key to get me through many challenges. I definitely needed to be placed with someone with a strong character because my behavior changes were only progressing at this point. I was misbehaving and acting out, as well as starting to take on different habits and friendships. My maternal grandmother sacrificed a lot to take care of me during that time of my life. She was dedicated to my care and well-being.

The school year wasn't over at that point so I had to attend fifth grade halfway through for a few months. My grandmother then got me into a nearby private school, Aberdeen Institute, where I entered sixth grade. I have a lot of good memories thanks to my time there. Despite all the wild, roller coaster changes, my years there were probably the happiest of my youth. I think a lot of it had to do with the fact that my grandmother gave me a lot of freedom. But everything comes at a price, and that freedom was no different…there was a price to pay.

I remember sitting down in the admissions office to take my entry test. Before I knew it, a kid the same age as me started taking the same test. We looked at each other— we couldn't talk. But we both knew that we wanted to do the same thing—copy each other's answers. But, of course, that was hard to do because there was always somebody there watching us. We clicked right away, and we started communicating with facial expressions and eye movements.

AND... SO WHAT? RESILIENCE THROUGH ADVERSITY

To this day we can understand that body language from each other. Funny thing is…I was never much of a dedicated student. But he didn't know that. Little did I know that 30 years later, Hector would remain one of my best friends. When the school year began, I was the first one seated in my class. The seat next to me remained empty until Hector walked in. He saw it and instantly sat down beside me. We were inseparable and became best friends, like brothers. There wasn't a teacher in sixth grade that didn't hate us. Needless to say, we had a blast! We engaged in all kinds of shenanigans and got in a lot of trouble, but that didn't stop us. We made cigarettes out of sheets of paper and baby powder. Before we knew it, everybody was doing it. There was baby powder all over the place! Other times, we sabotaged our classroom's musical recordings. During a recording of a Christmas song, we intentionally coughed and made all kinds of noises. We thought it was so hilarious. We would replay those recordings over and over again and just die laughing!

Sixth grade proved to be a good change for me in more ways than one. I had a loving grandmother. I had a place to live. And I started making friends. I was never very disciplined in school, but school provided me with the outlet to make friends, which is what I needed at the time. I needed companionship. I needed someone who understood me. As a result, in sixth grade I started to come out of my cage. I started to find support with my friends. I started to laugh more. At home, I had someone who loved me. All in all, I had care, some discipline, and a lot of fun.

I also made a lot of friends in my neighborhood. We were like The Goonies of Mexico City. Francois, Emilio, Hugo, Ana,

4. LIVING IN THE FAST LANE

and myself. We would get together at somebody's house and watch movies, play video games, and head out on excursions on our bikes. We rode everywhere. The freedom and the companionship were just what I needed. Those were such exciting times. But as we got older, our Goonies adventures morphed into serious partying. Looking back, we definitely started partying too early. I was thirteen or fourteen when I started smoking and drinking socially. At first, the parties were on select weekends. Over time they became what I did every weekend. I was always at someone's house, partying. We rarely partied at my house. My grandmother didn't approve. But sometimes, when she wasn't home, we would get together at my house to smoke cigarettes out the window while loud music was playing. One day my grandmother came home early from her eye-shopping walks at the local department stores and caught me and my two buddies Emilio and Francois. She quickly left the house and returned with three packs of cheap unfiltered cigarettes in hand.

"You guys are going to smoke the whole pack right now," she informed us. She gave us each a pack and would not leave until we each smoked the whole thing. We were grossed out by the time we did finish the pack, but the disgust eventually wore off, and a couple of days later we were back at it.

My grandmother tried to monitor me and would repeatedly tell me that she did not want me smoking. But there was only so much she could do. I would tell her that I wasn't smoking and not to worry as I took mints to hide the smell from her. But that wasn't all that I hid from her. My drinking also became more frequent and heavy until it got out of hand. I began excessively partying with many different

AND... SO WHAT? RESILIENCE THROUGH ADVERSITY

friends during the week, as well. I would come home at two or three in the morning. For better or for worse, there were no cell phones back then. I would just tell my grandmother where I would be and she would have to take my word for it. This is what I mean when I say that my freedom came with a price. Unfortunately, I did not understand that, and I paid the price.

As a result of all the partying, I paid less attention in school, and my already mediocre grades started to slip more and more. I was so consumed with partying and hanging out with my friends that I couldn't see anything else. That is when I began to have regular conflicts with my grandmother. We would argue a lot, day and night. My solution was to never be home. If I wasn't home, we wouldn't have arguments. It was difficult for me to understand that my behavior was causing the conflicts. Yet, I wanted to continue my behavior and not have the arguments.

I couldn't have both things. But I became very close with other friends at this point. They were my family because we shared similar pasts, troubled and conflicted. They knew what I was going through and passed no judgment, as well as requiring no discipline, which meant I could do whatever I wanted. And doing whatever I wanted meant going out to party and drinking—nothing productive. Just getting into whatever trouble crossed our paths.

It was around that time, in ninth grade, when I became very interested in music. So much so that Hector, my buddy Uriel, and I formed an alternative grunge band. It was very of-the-90s rock scene but a vibe ahead of its time. Our inspirations were Guns N Roses, Metallica, and Nirvana. Hector played

4. LIVING IN THE FAST LANE

bass, Uriel played guitar, Jorge was the vocalist, and I played the drums. Sadly, Jorge passed away right after high school. Interestingly, I had never played drums in my life. On top of that, everyone bought their own instruments except for me. I was broke, of course. It was nothing new back then. I didn't have 1,000 pesos just lying around. But one of my closest friends on the block was well off. His name was Francois. He came to Mexico City from France to learn Spanish and to go to school. He had a drum set; it was a brand new, blue New Beat set. Mind you, it was the cheapest drum set on the market but that didn't matter. What mattered was that there was no way I was going to say no to my friends. I needed to play in that band. So, I started going to Francois' house for jam sessions to learn the basics of drumming. Before long, I had learned how to play the basics. I figured I was ready to show off my skills to the band. But I still needed a drum set. I asked Francois if I could borrow his for a couple of days to practice with the new band. I laid it on thick how interested I was in playing with the band and how helpful it would be to practice the couple of songs we started composing as a band on his drum set. Francois said sure and even offered to drive the drum set over to band practice in his car as he was two years older than me. Then it came time for me to answer his question, "When will you get them back to me?" It was Monday so I said I would get them back to him by Friday.

Now, back then, I used to do a lot of things like that. Unfortunately that time was no different. It was definitely wrong of me. I will never deny it. But at that time, it was the answer— the drum set was a form of survival. The truth is… the drum set made me feel a part of something greater than life at the time. I could not risk not being part of the band. I could not risk my buddies not being my family. Otherwise, I was part of nothing again. I could not risk that. That thought alone brewed unbearable chaos in my head. So, I owed my band experience to Francois. The day he delivered the drums to the studio was the first time we had band practice together. Sadly, when Friday came I told Francois I would return the drum set the following week. When that week arrived, I told him there was no way I could return the drums because I had a gig. I promised him something that I knew I was not going to deliver. It wasn't in bad faith. I just could not give up on the experience and our dreams as a band because we were on to something great. Sadly, Francois never saw that drum set again in his life. I have since apologized and we both laughed about it. Francois and I are still good friends and remain in touch. When I think back on this now, I see that I not only stole someone's drum set, I also stole somebody else's desire, somebody else's dream. Sometimes what we have to do for survival is not necessarily something that will have positive long-term benefits. It's merely a quick fix. It's an interesting lesson to learn. Even though I ended up winning something in the short term, in the long run I endured some guilt and did something I wouldn't have done today.

Nevertheless, the band practiced regularly, and in not too much time we began playing at our party circuit. We had a lot of fun and had musical talent. But most of the time we would get drunk before the parties, so we sometimes sounded like shit. It didn't matter to us, though. People liked it. We also found the support and acceptance among us that we each so desperately craved. None of us had much of a male

4. LIVING IN THE FAST LANE

father figure constantly present, so our band became our brotherhood. There's a certain connection when you play music with someone and you both click. It was heaven. I loved it. I also think it was a connection that I was missing and that we were all missing. We spent hours playing in the studio, which was the service room of the seven-story building where Hector lived. It was at the very top of the building on the roof. We moved in before anyone could say no, and the first thing we did was spray paint everything. We spray painted the names of our favorite bands. We pinned Playboy posters all over the walls. It was our place where we hung out, created, and rocked out. Our songs were angsty, rageful, and protested everything we did not like.

We were called "Aire Muerto" which means "Dead Air." Even though the translation doesn't do any justice to the name, it was intended to be interpreted as a form of suffocation. We didn't take any crap from anyone. We recorded our songs on cassette tapes and an old tape recorder; it was quick and affordable. The quality was terrible, but we were thrilled to hear our own demos on tape. None of us had cars at the time, so to play our gigs we would pack up all of our instruments in the back of a taxi, which back then were mostly Volkswagen Beetles. We were packed like sardines, but we would make it all fit somehow. Drum set, guitar, bass, amps, plus three of us. We were just excited to make it to our next gig. We played concerts on the roof of a schoolmate's house. Slamming into each other during our sets, throwing our guitars and drum sticks, and usually participating in whatever fight broke out before the night was over.

Unfortunately, my wild times only accelerated from

AND... SO WHAT? RESILIENCE THROUGH ADVERSITY

there. I started skipping school when I was fifteen and sixteen years old. At that point my buddies and I were no longer riding our bikes but driving cars all over Mexico City on busy streets and out into the mountains on dusty dirty roads at the "Desierto de los Leones." My Aunt Carmen taught me how to drive stick when I was fourteen, and that began my love affair with cars. I loved the sound of the car changing gears. I could feel the adrenaline rush and I wanted more. So much so that my friends and I would take cars of people we knew in the neighborhood…or from in front of our families' houses…out for long, fast drives. We went on joyrides with some neighbors' cars, my grandmother's car, and Francois' uncle's car. We must have done this more than a handful of times. Whatever car we could get our hands on, we drove. The point of joyriding was to drive fast and to feel a rush of excitement. Otherwise, what would be the point of just going for a ride around the block? We wanted to go and be excited about it. Fortunately, nothing serious ever happened during those joyrides. But we came very close.

    Once, after cruising around after a party at three o'clock in the morning, three guys jumped out, one with a gun, and started chasing us. Francois was driving his 1984 Mustang—which I would eventually cause to burn some other night at a race track while I was driving. During the gun assault, I was in the back seat. Thankfully nothing happened to us. We were out in the wrong place, at the wrong time. But obviously, that didn't stop us. We kept pressing our luck. My friends and I must have been in about three or four car accidents. Once we smashed into a car in front of us. Another time we crashed into a street median. That one was quite funny.

4. LIVING IN THE FAST LANE

Francois was driving, another friend was in the passenger seat, and I was in the back seat with another friend. We were most likely on our way to a party. While making our way down a big avenue, a fork in the road appeared and a decision needed to be made. Francois called out, "Where am I going? Left or right?" The guy in the front yelled, "Right!" I screamed, "Left!" We went back and forth, "Right! Left! Right! Left!" Until Francois drove boom into the divider. We laughed so hard. We couldn't believe it!

Another accident involving a street median occurred when Hector and I were racing each other at midnight. We had found each other at a red light. What are the odds in such a big city! We started chasing each other for about ten minutes when he lost control of his car on a curve. He was going so fast that he jumped the center divider and smashed into a building on the other avenue, against opposing traffic. What was even scarier was that his car was full of people. Thankfully, there were only minor injuries even though the car was a total loss. Uriel was in the front passenger seat. He unfortunately broke his leg and Hector broke a front tooth. The three girls in the back seat were fine. I was in the other car with my girlfriend at the time and her sister. But that's how it was then. There's a car…there's a key…let's go! We were literally living in the fast lane.

School was in the rearview mirror. I was skipping school constantly. But it was no secret. My family would get the call from school. My paternal grandparents were now paying for the private school because my grandmother could not afford it, so they would get notified. My paternal aunt Raquel would then call me and I would totally lie. The truth was I was not going to school. My main goal at that time in life was to have a good time, and that's what I did. I had a girlfriend, I had friends, I partied, and I enjoyed the open road. I was enjoying my freedom. Up until that point I had felt so trapped with everything that happened before in my life. I wanted to escape and focus on doing things that made me get away from everything, and I mean everything! Skipping school and driving with my friends was one of the ways I could do that because it was exciting. It was new, and I was taking a lot of risks. But the reality was that I was lost. I didn't know what I was doing, why I was doing it, or where I was going. I was just living in that moment. I wasn't really thinking about what would happen if I flunked out of school. Nor did I spend any time thinking about my future. I was just thinking about the now. And I did not want to spend it alone or at home. Anywhere but home because home meant questions and control and I was fed up with both. I'd found my freedom, which was better than suppression and control.

My family was taking measures to keep me in check, but sometimes that meant closing doors on me because of my behavior. At that time, I didn't understand why I was doing what I was doing. But I also needed some kind of familial support. For example, I once took my uncle's car for a joyride. He was the husband of my aunt Raquel, who lived by my paternal grandparents. That joyride turned out to be a really bad idea because they found out and got really mad at me. So much so that they prohibited me from coming to the house. The thing is, I couldn't see through my needs at that time—the need for acceptance and freedom at all costs, which was something that had been taken from me at a very young age.

4. LIVING IN THE FAST LANE

I guess I was simply looking to belong and to fit in. For me that meant partying, music, friends, and girlfriends.

I was considered a bad boy at school, which gave me a great sense of security. In the past, weakness meant abuse and tragedy. Being the bad boy meant I was the center of attention and that I was in control. Being in control made me feel secure, strong, and gave me confidence, for all the wrong reasons. But when you're in survival mode, you do what you have to do to get through. Survival of the fittest, pretty much. To my knowledge and my ignorance, it was the best I could do at the time. It was not necessarily right or the best way. All I knew was I couldn't go back to being the weak guy getting bullied and abused. But we pay a price for everything, and so did I.

While I was popular at school, nobody really cared about me and my friends in the city. I never did anything wrong to anyone directly, but I think because of what people heard or saw, they had strong feelings about me. Once when my friend Francois and I were walking down the street near the high school, we encountered a group of kids that didn't like me. Not from the school but from the streets. We had it in for each other. We got into an argument. I had my pocketknife on the ready. I used to always carry a knife given the circumstances of my life at the time. One guy was carrying half of a broomstick and another had a gun. It did not look good at all. So I said, "What's it going to be? What do you want?" The guy then hit me in the face with his broomstick, claiming that I had been running my mouth with his girlfriend. I took two steps back to get my pocketknife out. As I stepped back, I almost tripped, which caused me to lose the knife. It was now on the ground! I rushed down to grab it, but I saw the guy already coming towards me with the stick for my head. Somehow, I grabbed the knife and swirled my body just enough to the left to avoid a major impact from the broomstick. It went through my arm. As I got up, the guy who had the gun lifted his shirt to show he was packing and said, "You guys need to calm down." My friend and I miraculously walked away alive. I just had a big bruise on my mouth. It wouldn't be the first one or the last one. Funny thing is…his girlfriend became my girlfriend a year later. Yes, life is funny sometimes.

 My grandmother noticed a lot of things, and she knew that I was going through a difficult time. I was already making a lot of bad decisions and there wasn't much more she could do so we clashed a lot. We had major arguments day in and day out. Then one day during one of our arguments she had a nervous breakdown. She started throwing and breaking things in her bedroom. I didn't know what was going on. I was so scared. I thought we were going back to 1987 when my mom died. The same feeling of emptiness in my stomach was back. My Aunt Carmen then came down to the house and realized that my grandmother was having a nervous breakdown. It was so bad that she had forgotten who we were. That's when I knew things were definitely getting out of hand. My grandmother was already an extremely nervous person. She worried a lot. I think she felt it was her duty to take care of me in the absence of my mom, her daughter. I think my mother's passing really affected her so much…like she lost a part of herself. She tried to take care of me the best she could, but with me going through wild transitions, it was very difficult.

4. LIVING IN THE FAST LANE

I was on a path of self-destruction but I didn't know it because I thought I was just having fun. At that point, I was frequently coming home late after partying with my friends. Looking back, my family had to find a way to get in the middle of my path in order for me to make a radical change in my life. They eventually called a meeting at my grandmother's house. It was about my future. Both sides of my family were there. They asked big questions, like "What do you want to do with your life? What do you want to see in your future?" I had no idea. I never thought beyond what I wanted to do in the moment. I said, "I want to be in a band. I'll be a drummer for the rest of my life." They replied hysterically, "Oh, my God, are you crazy?" I said, "No. That's what I want to do." Obviously, they did not entertain that idea for a second. Thankfully, they didn't because I don't think I would have lived this long if I had become a drummer at that rhythm of life.

My second idea—"I want to be a race car driver." They were floored, "Where is this coming from?" I thought I was really good at driving—on top of my close-call accidents—but never as a driver in those cases. Sometimes Hector would pick me up in his mom's car to do fast loops around a parking lot that was laid out as a track. I would drive around really fast. We loved it. One of my uncles replied, "You know that requires a lot of money. You are going to need a sponsor. Then you're going to have to get a team." Everybody looked at my uncle with obvious "shut-up-don't-encourage-him" stares. That was a big no.

Before I could think of a third idea, my family said," What about military school?' I didn't think twice—"That's

AND... SO WHAT? RESILIENCE THROUGH ADVERSITY

not happening in a million years." While it was a fast no for me, it was a fast yes for them. Their minds were already made up. I needed a drastic change.

I have a black eye from some fight. Dinner at a family gathering.

Picture taken at my paternal grandparents before going to Military school.

My best friend Hector and I rallying around dirt roads while ditching school.

5

"YES, SIR!"

"Learning discipline is like learning to ride a bicycle. You never forget it."

My emo, punk self, spent my junior year of high school at a military school in Virginia. The first 30 days were quite an adjustment. For starters, I had long hair, I wore dark clothes, and I had a dark attitude. I was the exact opposite of who you would picture in military school. Once there, my first stop was the barber shop. I told the guy, "A little bit here, a little bit there." The man just shaved my head. I couldn't believe it. "What are you doing?" Without skipping a beat he yelled back, "This is military school, boy!" I was definitely far from home. I was then off to pick up my uniforms, meet people, and register for this and that. The discipline was very intense and there was a fixed schedule for everything. I was in for a rude awakening. Literally.

The next morning at 6:15 a.m. a drill sergeant stormed into my room. There was a giant bell in the center of the barracks. He rang that bell repeatedly and screamed, "Wake up! Wake up! Wake up!" I was so disoriented. What the hell

5. "YES, SIR!"

was going on? Then we were informed that we had only 30 minutes to get ready, to take a shower, and to present ourselves at 7:00 a.m. formation. If we were late, we had to do push-ups. Getting ready entailed making sure our shoes were spit-shine ready, our brass was shiny, and our shirt and pants were presentable. Then we had to eat breakfast in the mess hall before going to our first class. School was in session until about two or three o'clock in the afternoon. We only had 30 minutes for lunch. But, before we got to eat lunch, we had to go to formation again. There was a process for everything. And that's how we learned discipline because we had no choice but to follow it. If we did not follow the rules, we would spend all of our free time doing push-ups and marching orders instead of getting to go into town to hang out with friends. The school was in a very small town so everybody knew Fishburne and it wouldn't take long for the townspeople to find out who we were if we did something wrong. So cadets always had to behave.

Needless to say, I was very depressed for the first 30 days. I felt completely out of place. I just didn't know what I was doing there. It hadn't sunk in yet. It was a tough lesson to learn. But I eventually applied the first lesson I learned after my mother died. You have to adapt to survive. So, I focused on doing that because I knew there was no way that I was going to survive by standing out from the 400 other boys in that military school. If I was going to make it, I had to be one of them. That meant I had to be tough. It meant I had to get used to my new surroundings. And it meant I had to try to do my best. I knew deep down inside that although I had lived a reckless life until that point, I had indeed always tried my best. Whether it was driving or playing drums or making music, I had always tried my best. Unfortunately, that wasn't always the case with school because that meant control. But everything that I was interested in I had put 150% effort into. Thankfully, for me, for some strange reason, I started to like military school. And I started to give it my best.

I thought the military formation drills with rifles were pretty cool. I also enjoyed the opportunities to play sports. I played soccer during the summer—I had always played soccer back home. During the winter months I was part of the wrestling team. Wrestling came natural to me because I was used to getting into fights all the time. But I now wanted to learn the technical ways to use that discipline, and I became really good at it. Altogether I think those activities started to motivate me and helped keep my mind away from worrying about what was going to happen next in my life and dwelling on how much I missed my friends, my girlfriend, and my life. I was too busy at that point and too involved with my new life at military school so that within 30 days my mindset started to change, really change. I actually started to like the discipline. I still wasn't doing great in my classes. But I was doing better, and I now had a special education tutor that helped me. I also started making friends.

I also began learning more about the kids I went to school with. Some of them had troubled legal pasts that had done some bad stuff, and I felt like I needed to watch my back. Fights broke out all the time, and some of the fights got out of hand. For instance, a kid got stabbed in the head during one of them. In another, a chair was smashed against a kid's back. There was also an underbelly of alcohol during

5. "YES, SIR!"

nonschool hours. In one kid's room there would be alcohol. In another kid's room somebody would be smoking weed. On the other side of the hall there would be two kids raving. And in another room the Confederate flag was hung on the wall as kids listened to metal music. The school was strict. There would be room checks daily, but those checks didn't catch everything. Weirdly, the school never said anything about the Confederate flag. I wondered sometimes if what I saw was just what those students wanted to represent or were they true believers in that flag. Did they really know what it meant? But if they did, wouldn't they not be my friends? It was weird. But I went along with things.

My English was getting better, but it still wasn't great. I had improved significantly given that I was practicing all day long. But you know how kids are. They can be cruel. And despite the diversity of the military school's students, racism still endured. Funny thing is, we all hung out together—Black, White, Chinese, Japanese, Mexican, and Puerto Rican—but stupid things were said all the time. I was called a beaner and a spic. But I really didn't take offense. I figured you could think whatever you wanted to think and say whatever you wanted to say—that was your choice. But then it was my choice to hear what I wanted to hear or not hear. At the end of the day, it didn't matter where you came from, what color you were, or what race you were. At the end of the day, you were in military school, and being the last man standing was what mattered there. That was something I learned to appreciate. I quickly saw that a lot of people talked tough but couldn't really support it. I didn't want to be one of those people. So I kept to myself, but stood up when it was necessary.

AND... SO WHAT? RESILIENCE THROUGH ADVERSITY

I got by, and my communication skills improved because in order to make friends I had to talk with people around me. So I adapted and I made a lot of friends. It was trial and error because there was also a rank system to consider. Just because some were younger than you didn't mean you could overlook them or try to boss them around. You had to respect them if they had a higher rank than you because they could order you around and make you march for hours. Military school was a different ecosystem. As a result, I learned to respect people. Not only because they were older but because they were people. Most importantly, I learned that respect is a two-way street, no matter your age or position in any ecosystem.

I also learned to appreciate people by their merits. I began to see how certain people didn't move up in rank while others moved up only to drop back down because they were screwing around. I was one of those that moved up in rank quite fast. That's because I didn't want to be pushed around. The entry level was called "rat." I didn't want to be anyone's rat. But that's not to say I didn't get into any fights to protect my dignity. You really couldn't help it in that type of environment. One of the kids would get on everyone's nerves; someone would then snap with a punch; and before you knew it, you were throwing punches, too. In that environment, being able to hold your own in a fight proved that you were not weak.

Whether you avoided punches or punched back, somebody had to be standing at the end. That's how respect was earned in military school. As a result, you learned to stand up for yourself. This discipline also showed us that life is going to throw shit at you and you are going to have to

5. "YES, SIR!"

learn how to deal with it no matter what. I had been through that before. So I was like, "OK, I think I can do this. I need to step up my game. I need to do what I need to do to get my rank up." And that's what I did. I was in it to win it.

I improved my grades, in part thanks to a teacher that I admired a lot because I found him so intriguing. He was older, probably in his 70s, and he had a very unique personality and character. He had lost an eye in the Vietnam War and wore a patch that he made fun of from time to time. And, when he spoke, he whispered mysteriously. He taught English mostly and focused a lot on poetry. He loved Poe's "The Raven." He was very kind and very funny. I looked up to him and his endurance. This man had flown planes in combat and survived. The things he must have seen, the pain he must have withstood, and the strength he must have needed to survive—and here he was with all of us, giving us his time and knowledge. I admired his resilience.

In addition to doing better in school, I also joined the marching band as a drummer. This time I wasn't sitting and playing the drums. I was standing. I was carrying the snare drum. We marched down the streets and during parades with the school around different cities, sometimes competing with other military schools. People in the town would watch us and clap, and it was fun. I also got to travel with the band and perform in parades in different towns throughout Virginia. It was an amazing experience.

Traveling on my own would turn out to be an unexpected perk of military school. My family insisted that I stay in the States during school breaks and holidays. It was a little disappointing at first. But then it also meant freedom. I decided to travel. I asked my friends in school, "Hey, I have nowhere to go. Can I go with you?" There were so many options! I traveled all over by bus. I visited Kentucky, Indiana, Pennsylvania, Cincinnati, Washington, D.C., and Los Angeles. I even went to the White House where I snuck my camera inside the security bars and took a picture. Those were the days. It was a lot of fun! I was very lucky to have friends at the time whose families allowed me to spend time with them and to join them for the holidays. Traveling also opened my eyes to see how people lived in certain areas. Looking back, I didn't understand why my family didn't want me to go back to Mexico City to visit. I can see now that it was best for me to stay where I was. They did not want to interrupt the new path that I was on. They wanted me to stay through the whole experience and perhaps not fall back into old habits.

One of my biggest accomplishments was receiving the Presidential Fitness Award signed by President Bill Clinton. That accomplishment was tough. There were a number of requirements to accomplish in order to receive that award. Out of 400 kids, only five of us got it. We had to run a mile within seven minutes and do a certain number of push-ups and pull-ups, and it was hard.

I also received a couple of medals and ribbons, including a medal of conduct, which blew my mind. I had never behaved in my life! The medals and ribbons inspired me to keep pursuing that path and to keep excelling. I had a great year at that school.

But my time would prove to be limited. I wanted to go back for my senior year and graduate from military school—I ended up liking it so much. But my family couldn't afford

5. "YES, SIR!"

another year due to the currency depreciation in Mexico. And military school wasn't cheap. It was a private school tuition that some of my family members chipped in to pay for, so I am eternally grateful for such an amazing experience. I grew up significantly—mentally, physically, and spiritually—during that year. I matured so much. I learned the meaning of discipline and how to stand up for myself with bravery and strength. I have really great memories of that school. More importantly, I think a seed was planted for a major tipping point that took me in a different direction.

Marching at military school.

Enjoying a car show outside the military school.

Marching at military school.

Cadet Villegas - Military School.

6

CRASH LANDING

"When you hit rock bottom, the best view is looking up and onward."

I went back to Mexico City in 1996 to live with my maternal grandmother once again. I was seventeen and I felt lost. The discipline I had learned in military school was there, but so were my friends that I had missed. I had a nice reunion with my neighborhood friends. It was really good to see everybody. Francois was back visiting from France, and we hung out like our old Goonies days. But the itch for my old lifestyle was strong. I eventually went back to partying, and I was quickly dragged back into stupid fights. At that point, I did not want to fight. I really wasn't interested. But it was all-consuming in my environment and that's where my friends were.

    I also faced a setback. My high school refused to validate my study abroad in military school so I had to repeat the eleventh grade. Unfortunately, that wasn't the first time I was held back. I had to repeat the third grade after my mother died. Needless to say, I was very disappointed that time around. But I still set my goals. I was going to hit the books

6. CRASH LANDING

and graduate. To help pay for that extra year of school, my uncle Raul offered me a part-time job in exchange for paying for the school's tuition. I thought it was a fair trade at the time, but looking back, my uncle paid more for my school than I had worked. That year, I went to school from 7:00 a.m. to 2:00 p.m., and then worked at my grandfather's shop from 3:00 p.m. to 7:00 p.m. I went home by metro and bus, did homework, and did it all over again the next day and the day after that.

   I didn't have access to a car at that time, so I was either taking the bus or taking the metro. In the beginning I didn't mind this so much. But then I began to feel a little left out because a lot of my friends had cars of their own. I saw them driving around while I was on the bus and I started to feel different. I tried to stay disciplined with school but my social life finally won out. My uncle would ask me, "Why are your grades dropping? You went to military school." I noticed that my grades were slipping, too, but I also knew that my friends were still very important to me despite being away for a year. The band tried to get back together, also…but without a drummer. It was Hector and me, recording acoustic guitar versions of our songs. My grandmother gave Francois' drum set away to the trash person while I was at military school. I couldn't believe it. "You could have asked me," I said. She reminded me that the drum set hadn't technically cost me anything. My grandmother knew that I had taken the set from my friend. Life has a way to get you eventually. What comes easy, goes easy. So now when we got together to jam, I just played guitar, sang, and recorded. Nothing as serious as before.

   But I needed more distractions. My good friend Hector

and I began making prank calls using street pay phones. Hector knew my past, so we started to call Juan. The phone number had not changed all those years. We were in luck! I now had anger against him and against what he had done to my mother and me. I figured I'd prank him for the rest of his life. We called him frequently just to annoy the hell out of him. He was definitely sick and tired of us calling. I don't know why he never changed his phone number. But that was nothing compared to what he had done to my past. The prank calls gave me some satisfaction.

Around that time Hector got a car, another great distraction. We would drive around, meet people, and hang out. My grades again continued to drop and my family worried some more.

I seemed to do so well in military school—why was I going back into what I was doing before? Well, for starters, I wasn't in military school anymore. Things were different back home. I was diverting into what I was doing before without even noticing it. In fact, a couple of times when my grandmother went out of town, I had huge parties at the house with 100 people in attendance. There would be kids passed out on the floor and broken glass everywhere. I don't know how we pulled it off, but somehow we managed to get it all cleaned up before she got home. To this day I don't know why the neighbors never said anything to her. Those parties were so bad. It was insane!

Despite it all, I finished my junior year of high school. Then all hell broke loose during my senior year. I was trying to cope with everything. I was trying to be what people wanted me to be. The expectation was that I had been rehabilitated

6. CRASH LANDING

in military school and that I was more responsible now. But I was emotionally struggling and the reality was that no one knew. Everyone thought I was rebellious and irresponsible. I was seventeen years old and couldn't be held accountable for anything. I couldn't keep those distractions going anymore. As a result, I started spending a lot of time alone and became very depressed. I didn't know what I was supposed to be doing or what I was doing with my life. The question suddenly lingered again in my head. I had no purpose.

    I tried to cope with school, and I kept going. I kept playing soccer, but I wasn't fully into it. My group of friends had changed. Hector and I lost touch during my senior year. He was now in a different school. My friends on the block were not the same. Some had moved or moved on. The relationship with my girlfriend was full of drama. Everything just felt different, and I started to feel very lonely. I felt that my life was falling apart and I wasn't ready for it. It took an emotional toll on me, and I had no haven. I couldn't focus in school, and my grandmother and I were bickering and fighting all the time. I had hit rock bottom again. I was back to square one.

    I started to write a lot during that time. A lot of song lyrics, poems, and my thoughts on any piece of paper I could find. I went from spending all of my time out with friends to sitting at home in my room. My grandmother noticed I was going through something but didn't know how to deal with it. I didn't know how to deal with it, either, so maybe it was for the best that she didn't get too involved. I wouldn't have been able to answer any of her questions. All I knew was that I felt empty inside. I felt a void. I think I was finally beginning to

AND... SO WHAT? RESILIENCE THROUGH ADVERSITY

feel the loss of my mother in my loneliness. It was devastating. All those years I had been trying different ways to escape that reality emotionally, but the list of distractions got longer and longer. Alcohol, smoking, friends, girlfriends, partying, cars, the band, anything that took me away from myself. But eventually it hit me. There was nothing I could use or do or say that would distract me anymore. I came to the realization that, emotionally, my mother was gone. And that's when the loss and grief of my mother sank in, and I became extremely depressed. Especially within the culture that I lived in. Depression was not something that people talked about. It wasn't really considered as something serious. It took me years to understand that I had gone through a major depression. It's very hard to address something you don't understand. As a result, I went through the motions for many months. I slept, drank, wrote, and it became a very dark time.

The last year of high school was very challenging as a result. I thought I was never going to make it. My depression blurred any desire that I might have had for anything. It also wore me down and I couldn't focus on anything else. My mind was literally a mess and my grades were horrible as a result. I had to take two or three tests over just to be able to pass those classes and graduate. My prom was short-lived and I ended up going alone. After I finished high school, my family insisted that I go on to university. I wasn't too keen about that, but I went along. I took a couple of admissions exams with the least interest of anything I've ever done in my life. I literally hoped I would not get into any of those schools because the concept just felt so alien to me. I wasn't in the right mind, place, or space. College was not going to

6. CRASH LANDING

work for me at that time. As hard as I pushed myself to try to do something, I knew I just couldn't. I was right. I ended up never hearing back from any of the schools I took exams for, and I didn't care.

I decided to get a job after high school, so I started working at the mall with a friend of mine at a small kiosk selling cell phone accessories such as batteries, leather covers, and chargers. It gave me something to do, and it was fun. My friend and I joked and fooled around a lot and played stupid games in between selling merchandise. It distracted me for a while. During that time, Motorola and Nokia were all the rage and cell phones were the size and weight of bricks. Unfortunately, that job only lasted a few months and my depression was still going strong, unknowingly. I still didn't know what I wanted to do with my life. The questions "who am I?... what am I here for?...what's my purpose?" began circling in my head like a broken record. I had to suffer through before I could get to my next step.

One day my friend at work came to me and said he had an uncle out in L.A. who was looking for someone to help him with his business selling cell phone accessories and other related gadgets. I thought, sure, why not? I had family relatives I could stay with there and I didn't have any other plans. It also gave me the opportunity to get away from my boring routine and going to work with my friend's uncle for a couple of months and figuring out what I was going to do with my life. Without hesitation, I called my paternal uncle in L.A. and said, "Hey, I have great news. I'm going to live with you. I'm arriving on September 26." I had no idea for how long or any other details beyond that. I just knew I was headed his way no matter what. Otherwise, I'd figure out where to stay. I desperately had to do something about my life. I took a leap of faith and jumped in the water! As mentioned before, my first few years were very much a struggle, trial and error, but I always remained solid in my goals and my hard work to move forward. That would eventually pay off.

7

FRESH START

"Sometimes reinventing oneself is not a matter of choice; it is simply a must."

While that cell phone job never panned out, it got me to Los Angeles, where my new life began. There was definitely "no turning back." Arriving in Los Angeles at the age of nineteen years old, going through the experience of navigating various setbacks and moves, was not an easy task. But it definitely took me places I never expected to be and gave me many wonderful experiences that I will always cherish. Living through those challenges set me up for new opportunities in the long run. During those early college days when I first started going back to school more seriously, I made a new friendship with Carlos. And thanks to that new friendship, I landed a career job right out of college. Carlos didn't care that I didn't have my college degree in hand yet. He just wanted someone to fill the marketing job at the company he managed, and marketing is what I studied. I jumped from a clerical position at a hospital to becoming a marketing director at a rehabilitation hospital.

7. FRESH START

All the hustle I had done to survive since my arrival in Los Angeles prepared me for this moment. This was my time to shine. In the streets, you can't not know something. You can't be the weak one and not know how to respond or how to confront a situation. You just do what you have to do. So I applied for the job with that same philosophy and rocked the interview. It went something like this:

"How are you going to sell our services?"

I had no idea. I didn't know what services to use or which patients were going to use this level of care. "Anything is sellable. You can sell somebody a bag of sand. People will buy anything if you know how to sell it," I replied.

He liked my answers so much that my salary instantly doubled! I was hired! Now I needed to get the job done. I entered an industry I really had no knowledge of. I spent hours studying terms, codes, abbreviations, and lingo. It was a lot, but I had to learn fast so I could apply them.

I don't believe in faking it until you make it. You have to know what you are making and have your vision and a goal in mind. I was there for a year and then I jumped for an opportunity in the same position at another company that was a bit bigger and paid more. I was also there for a year before I jumped for another opportunity at a bigger chain. From there, everything took off. I was there for five years. That place was huge, just where I needed to be to scale up in my career. That was a great opportunity where I was also hired on the spot.

So much so that I developed a very unique program that didn't exist in Los Angeles. It was for patients that needed dialysis and certain services that couldn't be done in-house. I put the logistics together to enable them to be transported to a facility that could help them. The program became very successful. Unfortunately, towards the end of my time with that company, there was a change in management and I became unhappy with the direction of the company and where it was headed. But true to form, this presented me with another opportunity. An opening at one of the most well-known hospitals in L.A. I jumped ship and just in time. As soon as I left, the company went bankrupt nationally.

    At that point, I had gained a lot of experience in the medical field and in the marketing side of the industry. But I didn't necessarily know the acute hospital services setting so I had to learn fast again. Thankfully, I had a very good mentor to help. He was the chief of staff of the hospital. After some time there, he began planting a seed in me to start my own consulting company. He invited me to consult for the hospital, as well as an internal medical group, and vowed to not hold me exclusive. Once I figured out what that meant, I went for the challenge. I knew that he respected me and had my best interests at heart. And he was right. It opened up a whole new world of opportunities. I created my first corporation in 2013, and I consulted for the hospital, for the medical group, for doctors and for other facilities. I helped them market their services and in some cases took on revitalizing their customer service operations. Without good customer service, my marketing efforts would be inconsequential. I was busy, but I was single so I didn't care. I have since expanded my operations in various sectors of the industry. A couple of years ago I branched into launching

7. FRESH START

my own line of health supplements. During the COVID-19 pandemic, my company was fortunate enough to not have to close its doors like so many other businesses did. Instead, my firm had the opportunity to assist in providing protective supplies to various people in need. We were privileged to have worked with a recognized judge and other political figures to provide supplies to the city of Los Angeles and the homeless population of an important institution of downtown L.A. We also provided supplies to doctors' offices and other important health care entities.

    As I was making my way up the corporate ladder, I got my financial bearings, which led to more stability and independence in my life. So much so that in 2009, I took advantage of the low interest rates after the real estate bubble burst and bought my own house. I have since been able to invest in the real estate market over the years, which has given me a great deal of knowledge to be able to grow in that exciting industry. I have also been very fortunate to have traveled a great deal. In 2009, I visited Thailand and Cambodia for the first time. I also traveled through Europe, reunited with my childhood friend Francois and his wife and children in the small town where they lived, and saw the sites of Paris and other amazing cities around France. I went on to Spain where I backpacked through Barcelona, explored the great food, the city, and its beaches, before flying north to Santander, next to Bilbao, to see my paternal relatives who I had never met before. Then I also stopped in Madrid for a few days where I visited my cousin Daniela and her husband. In all, I explored and got lost in the wonder of the cities I visited; I ate delicious foods; I saw the amazing sites; I rode a motorcycle around Barcelona; and I did whatever I wanted to do. I had my complete independence, and I cherished it. It had been a long time coming.

    Aside from what I have been able to achieve in terms of professional success, the most important aspect of my success has been the ability to determine who I am and who I have become—a question that roamed in my mind for decades. I have a sense of accomplishment with myself—the fulfillment of knowing that I am capable of great things and even better than I ever imagined. My circumstances did not determine an excuse for failing my own self. With that in my mind and heart, now I am able to give back what I have learned and earned through my own sweat and tears. The best part is that I get to choose who I give back to and I also get to share that emotion and satisfaction. I'm not talking about materials or money. I'm talking about my most valuable asset—my time.

Las Vegas, with my cousin.

My best friend Hector and I during one of my many visits to Mexico City. Just catching up!

N.Y.

Pie de Concha - Spain 2009 Visiting what is left of a church from the late 1800's.

Pie de Concha - Spain 2009. This is the original place where my grandfather stems from. The root of my heritage.

Versailles. Visit with Francois, childhood friend.

Visting France in 2009.

Las Vegas. Francois visiting The United States.

Santillana del Mar, Spain 2009.

France Air Museum 2009. The Concord.

Riding my Harley up in the mountains in California.

Cambodia – Angkor Wat 2008.

Harley Adventures on the road. San Diego.

Checking out the bike before a trip up the coast.

Project car - Alfa Romeo 1987 - This car kept me busy for a very long time.

I'm getting my first tattoo. Not the last one either.

My Mother in Santillana Del Mar, Spain - 1979.

Santillana Del Mar, Spain - 2011 - Image taken by me. (32-year later)

Fun Fact: This image similarity and coincidence was discovered in the year 2021 while writing this book. I never knew my mother had visited that place. I could have never imagined I would take almost the same exact picture 32 years later and discover such a thing 41 years later.

My family, Sam, Rex and my wife. They made it all happen for me.

8

PROCESSING IT ALL

"Life lessons manifest in various ways. You can choose to make them learning experiences instead of repeating disappointments."

While I had achieved financial stability, I still struggled in the relationship department. I was now in my thirties and finally wanted to settle down and find a partner. I instead faced an emotional rollercoaster that lasted from 2009 to 2015. I dated a lot, never more than one woman at a time, but they all followed the same pattern, and I always felt a huge loss when they didn't work out and a depression would ensue.

We would date for a couple of months and then some kind of disaster would hit. We'd get into a big fight. Other times there would be disagreements I couldn't see past. It became like clockwork…relationship after relationship, disappointment after disappointment. At some point I thought to myself "something's going on here." I began to see a pattern of things starting off very well but then crashing right away. I then dug further into the background of the women I was dating and found another pattern—they

8. PROCESSING IT ALL

all seemed to share a troubled past of dysfunctional families. I realized that there was an issue and that I couldn't fix other people. But then how would I get out of the dating rut because it was constant? At some point the patterns became so blatant and repetitive that I became more skeptical. The signs were there, and I couldn't dismiss them. Something needed to change.

I started looking for help. It wasn't easy because you have to become very vulnerable in order to open up to a health professional. I wasn't really ready at that point to talk about my past with somebody that I didn't really trust. But a funny thing happened—I realized that the more I talked about my childhood trauma, the less complicated it became. It was evident that there was a connection in my emotional state between the tragic passing of my mother and the women I was dating. I pursued various forms of therapy. First, I worked with a psychologist who used stimulation to help me change my pattern of thinking and imagine different outcomes. I also did summer hypnosis therapy sessions. They all started to help a little, and I could feel the difference. However, I was still having trouble with the women that I was dating. So, I started to focus more on myself on top of seeing a therapist once a week.

I decided that I also needed to do my own therapy. I bought a Harley Davidson Sportster 882. It was a beauty. I took long midnight rides by myself. I found them to be very therapeutic and ironically relaxing. I would ride from Downey in Los Angeles to Oxnard along the Pacific coast. It was about a beautiful three-hour ride both ways. At that time of night, I didn't have to worry about too many drivers or traffic. It was just me, my bike and music in my headphones, cruising through the lonely night for hours. I made those night rides all year round. Sometimes they would be freezing, other times steaming during the day. It became some sort of a therapy for me because it required me to give 100% of my attention to the road. During those late hours on my bike, I didn't have to think about anyone, anything, or any situations. I could just go on for hours and turn off my mind for a bit. This process really helped me to think fresh and clear when it was time to resolve the areas of concern I was dealing with.

    I continued to use my financial resources to help me during my emotional roller coaster. In addition to riding my Harley, I created my own projects to work on at home. I bought an older 1991 Jeep Wrangler and started fixing it up. I worked on that project car for a while. I only knew basic mechanics, but that was enough to immerse my mind into those projects when I really needed time to turn off the noise in my head. I would focus my mind on figuring out how to remove the Jeep's alternator or the car's radiator instead. This process of taking out, putting back, replacing, and rebuilding vehicles really helped me a lot to centralize my focus and energy on positive and constructive thinking.

    I then discovered a self-development group that I was referred to by a friend of a friend. I wasn't really sure what to expect, but I spent a long weekend with 30 other people for three days of seminars that averaged about ten hours a day. It was very intense, and I had never done anything like it.

    The participants were anywhere from eighteen to 67 years old and everyone was going through similar experiences—

8. PROCESSING IT ALL

pain and grief because of traumatic experiences that had occurred at different points in their lives. The instructor was an amazing but tough middle-aged woman. She led us through various exercises and explained how the mind works and how we all perceive things differently. For example, as simple as when you see the color green, that might be the color blue for me. Or what you think is OK may not be OK with me. This can turn into very complex scenarios to say the least. In all, the importance of accepting what is rather than what you think it should be. As human beings, it is in our nature to want to be right. Instead, this translated into living in the present to the best of one's abilities. Accept what is. It's that simple. But to be able to live in the present, you have to let go of the past. Sure, but how do I do that? For many, many years, I went around carrying my backpack of trauma with me, 500 pounds of pain that I blamed everyone for. I acted the way I did because my mom died—because this happened or because that happened. I became so attached to that backpack, to that way of thinking, that it became my excuse as to why I was the way I was. It was through this group that I began to understand things about my life that I hadn't otherwise understood before. It also became clear to me that trauma is something that happens to everybody, not just me. In fact, just about everyone has gone through something, perhaps even right now, or has gone through a tragic experience, or will go through something at some point in their lives. Every person's timeline is bound to hit those barriers. What really matters is how we process this information. That part is really up to oneself.

    I remember the second day very clearly. One seminar

AND... SO WHAT? RESILIENCE THROUGH ADVERSITY

in particular really got to me. The instructor went around the room asking everyone, "Why are you here?" As people answered, it seemed to become a competition of sorts—the "who's got it worse?" contest. It also became apparent that we were all carrying baggage and struggling with our loads. Then the instructor pointed at me. It was my turn to answer "why are you here?" She also asked me, "What have you been dragging to this place?" I explained that I had a very traumatic childhood. That I was physically abused. That my mother was abused. That we had lived through hell with a man who beat her and me all the time. Then I started to go on a roll. It was like a snowball rolling down a snowy mountain. It just kept getting bigger and bigger and bigger. As the words poured out of my mouth, I began to notice that I was feeling an avalanche coming down on me. I then heard myself say, "Yeah, and then she committed suicide."

At that point, the instructor interrupted me with the most serious look on her face. She then peered into my eyes and said, "And so what?" There was only silence. All the breath in my body escaped me in that one quick moment. She completely disarmed me. I had no idea what to say in response because I had nothing left to say after that. I had nobody to blame, no excuse to justify my story or respond to her well-calculated question. I couldn't talk anymore and the room fell quiet.

In a split second the trajectory of my life and my perspective changed on account of three words, "And so what?" That's because I realized I had been the victim to the circumstances around me. I was telling my story to sell my story, to make people understand me. Yes, I've lived through

8. PROCESSING IT ALL

that. Yes, I've gone through that. But it doesn't mean that I still have to live the present with the past emotions on my back. It doesn't mean that I have to live by those rules or live by those thoughts. The circumstances won't determine who I am or who I am going to be. The mentality that I've been a victim before and so I am a victim now and I will be a victim in the future no longer had any power over me.

Changing that mentality allowed me to accept things for what they were and are and not what I wanted them to be. I always had a choice. A new way of thinking set in my mind. It changed my world around. Dating began to become less important, and the thought settled in that it doesn't have to work out. And if it doesn't work out, fine. Simply move on. I began to see that my life could keep moving forward positively despite my traumatic upbringing and that I was not attached to the victimization of the circumstances I suffered as a child. That my life keeps moving forward.

I then completed a seven-day retreat out in the mountains with the same group. That one was a bit more intense. It focused on facing fears and challenging yourself through difficult times using some physical exercises. For example, I climbed a 40-foot pole. I still can't believe I did that. Once I reached the top I had to figure out how to stand on top of the pole and jump to grab a handlebar about 6 feet away from the pole. I was hitched to ropes for my safety, but all the mobility, agility, and strength needed to complete that exercise were up to me. That retreat worked out really well. I think I needed that extra push to recharge my self-confidence.

I met my wife one year later in the Redondo Beach metro station. Funny thing is that I had rarely rode the metro at that point. But I was riding it that day because I had left my car at the dealership next door and I just wanted some time to keep practicing my positive thinking. I had noticed her on the platform, but I had my headphones on and was listening to music while I waited for the train. When it arrived, I stepped in and sat down, ready to go home. Then I felt a tap on my shoulder. It was my wife. She asked me how to get to Willowbrook station. I actually didn't know but I offered to look at the map with her. After we figured out where she was going, we got to chatting. She was from the Ukraine and was in Los Angeles for three or four days to take a medical exam to become a doctor. I told her I was in the business side of the medical field, too. We couldn't believe how much we had in common, but she seemed skeptical. We had the chance to hang out for the next two days before she went back to Ukraine. I took her where she wanted to go—the Observatory, the Walk of Fame, Hollywood, and the Chinese Theater. We exchanged numbers and remained in communication for the next several months. I then decided to visit her in Ukraine where I spent a couple of weeks abroad. I had the opportunity to meet her mother who was very sweet to me but also vetted me throughout my stay. She was a blast. It was quite an experience.

A year later, we got married in Las Vegas where we had an amazing time. We are very fortunate to have a very peaceful life together…that we share with our 90-pound pit bull, Rex. I couldn't have asked for a better partner. My wife is now expecting our first child, and we are so excited to start a new chapter in our lives. It is a surreal feeling to know that I will be having a child, despite the life I have lived. I am witness

8. PROCESSING IT ALL

to what I don't want my child to ever go through. May God give us the time and wisdom to always provide what I lacked. Unconditional LOVE.

Looking back, it's almost unbelievable the amount of hurdles, tragedy, and pain I had to endure to be able to make it to a stable point in my life. It has been quite an unexpected and eventful journey, but I have kept pushing to get to this point. I can firmly state that nothing was given to me on a silver platter. All the struggles I have endured in the process of my life have made me appreciate what I have accomplished. None of it was free. I paid the price from an early age through rejection, physical abuse, and abandonment and through many years of struggle trying to understand who I was.

For many years, I looked at my glass half empty. Not because I was in a negative state of mind, but sometimes that was all I had. It is easy to lose hope in desperate times, and the easy alternative would have been to become complacent, lazy, and make excuses for failing my own self. There were many dark days and lonely nights when I wasn't sure if I would make it the next day. Life was rough, always teaching me a tough lesson that I wasn't yet ready to learn. In a natural process of growth, this analogy has great wisdom—in order for a fruit to ripen, it must go through time, growth, and struggle so that at some point the fruit will reach maturity. It is with this same idea that I compare my growth. I reached my emotional maturity to overcome my biggest loss at 38. It took me 30 years to process all that had happened to me. My glass is now half full.

Myself jumping from a 40ft pole. Testing my fears.

Taking a dessert trip in California.

My wife and I visiting Los Cabos.

Coffee with Krystyna, my wife while we were dating. Ukraine 2015.